Be Serious: Essays by Stephanie Hayes

Be Serious: Essays by Stephanie Hayes

Stephanie Hayes

Creators Publishing
Hermosa Beach, CA

BE SERIOUS: ESSAYS BY STEPHANIE HAYES

Cover art by Little Shiva

CREATORS PUBLISHING
737 3rd St
Hermosa Beach, CA 90254
310-337-7003

ISBN (print): 978-1-962693-91-2

First Edition
Printed in the United States of America
1 3 5 7 9 10 8 6 4 2

A Note From the Publisher

Our goal is to make you think. We want you to react. We want you to respond.

Since 1987, the writers we represent and publish start discussions, arguments and even controversies. Love them or hate them, you can't ignore them.

Beginning with print and evolving into digital, Creators has been at the forefront of the media industry. We have been disrupting the status quo since our company was founded on the premise that creators should own their work, characters and ideas. Decades later, we continue to evolve as society pushes forward and technology changes.

At Creators, we support creators.

—Creators Publishing

Contents

Introduction

I shuffled down the pedestrian trail in my Florida neighborhood trying to avoid wayward droplets of saliva that might kill me. My ambling was punctuated by hee-honk ugly crying, the kind of sniveling in which the nostrils flare and the chin quivers and one's rosacea hits a vessely inflection point.

What have I done? I thought. *WHAT HAVE I DONE?*

It was March 2020; you may now pause for a knowing sigh. A few months earlier, before a raging virus held the world hostage, I made the foolish mistake of soul-searching. Never do this! What soul-searching does is cause people to abandon comfort in search of creative fulfillment, which almost always ends in credit card debt. In December 2019, I'd decided I wanted to change my job. I was working as an editor at the Tampa Bay Times, a lovely role in which I got to say things like, "I think you can sharpen your point here," or, "Just have fun with it!" before hustling off to meetings in stylish managerial outfits.

I'd always harbored a desire to write humor pieces. I envisioned a recurring feature that was not overtly political, but rather, leaned more personal. I wanted to comment on life in Florida, on the larger culture, on current events, and above all, on the simple, absurd act of existence. The idea seemed reasonable then. Of course, the world was always filled with chaos. But we were still in "precedented" times, if you will, not yet aware of the tragic loss, conspiratorial mistrust and existential reset waiting around the corner.

My boss liked the idea for the column, so I sketched out potential topic ideas including "Floribama Shore and the persistence of memory" and "Is this bug normal?" We agreed I'd start writing cheeky commentary in... yes. March 2020. On my last day as an editor, Times reporters were seeking information about the first case of COVID-19 in Florida.

So, flash forward to the dreaded nature trail. My husband and I had canceled a vacation and started a new life growing scallions in mason jars. My new job didn't start for two weeks.

That meant I had nothing to do except watch various HGTV shows in which Canadians renovated houses for passive-aggressive couples. That and feel nauseous. The Centers for Disease Control advised that walking, so long as you carried a 12-foot PVC pole to bat away strangers, was fine.

Away from the bleating confessional cries of, "We just need more room to entertain," I thought through my task. How was I going to make jokes during this, one of the most tragic global events in recent history? I was sure to offend people, say the wrong thing. This turned out to be an informative fear to work through fast. I soon realized there is no such thing as pleasing everyone, and some days, there is no such thing as pleasing anyone!

The answer was disturbingly clear and murky at the same time. I didn't have to have answers, but I did have to move forward. To be a human and write honestly. There was no other way out of the uncertainty than through it.

I, by then a real-life Victor Hugo character, pulled myself together and trudged home. I opened the laptop on my couch and started writing:

"I have not worn makeup in six days," I wrote. "I have turned into Reek from 'Game of Thrones.'"

And:

"Last night, we walked to a tiny park down the street. A woman was walking her dog, a dopey-looking Boston Terrier. The dog was wearing a purple necktie. He looked like he had just come from a long day at the office in 1974."

And:

"I'm not sure how I fit into this moment, or how jokes and lighter-side columns work right now. I guess we're going to find out together."

I pulled this together into something 70 percent cohesive and released it to the world. And I heard nice things from people, folks who were feeling just as awkward and afraid and unsure of what to say or do as I was. Of course they were. Of course.

Those ghastly times have waned, and for better or worse, new writing fodder has emerged. The preponderance of material remains especially high in Florida, a deeply unserious, lawless land governed by guys doing backflips off boats after drinking ten White Claws. People from all over the country flooded this state during the pandemic, as if we could possibly handle seeing any more people from Michigan attempt to pair bikinis with Crocs.

All of us have, in these last few years, lived through chaotic elections, necessary racial reckonings, an attempted government coup, too many shootings to count, the reversal of reproductive rights, a popcorn of presidential indictments, natural disasters, book banning, retrograde moral panic. We've learned terms like "crypto" and "Chat GPT" and "metaverse." We millennials were informed that our side-parted hair and skinny jeans were over and that we were now tragically disgusting.

The short essays in this collection will take you on a journey through these memories and more. We'll visit the moments when we were still waiting on vaccines, when we had to follow one-way tape arrows through grocery stores. We'll relive the innocent era before Elon Musk bought Twitter, or whatever Twitter is called now, in the manner the rest of us spontaneously buy a new pair of whimsical shoes lacking arch support.

While my work has grown more political over the years out of necessity – avoiding politics is like trying to take a bathroom selfie and keep the toilet out of the shot – I've stayed close to my mission of being irreverent. The layer of levity makes the serious people yell at me to be more serious, as if I am Spider-Man and I, alone, can save the subway car full of children from falling off the track. I've also written serious takes plenty of times, which makes the funny fans yell at me to just be funny.

What I am trying to tell you is this: My inbox, though overwhelmingly a Good Place, can sometimes devolve into the very fever dream I'd once feared, full of disembodied, yelling mouths, proverbial saliva droplets flying. But as I always dreamed, the work is consistently fun. And it's exciting. And challenging. And, I regret to inform you fellow soul-searchers, it's creatively fulfilling.

Sometimes, I close the laptop and let a hush fall over the room so I can more clearly hear the designers on HGTV discuss why an old, rusted bicycle would make chic wall decor. Then I'll step outside and wander onto that very walking trail where I scared the townspeople years ago. I'll take a deep breath with a steady chin. And I'll think, *If I'm being serious, it's all good.*

Be Relevant

Kohl's Is Trying to Kill Me

Nov. 26, 2022

Picture me at the Kohl's register about to lose my last two marbles, moments away from being enshrined on the internet as a lady who has melted down inside a Kohl's on a Friday night when she should be doing anything else with her one wild and precious life. Yet here she is. In Kohl's.

I hate Kohl's! And it's not like, "Oh, please, what did Kohl's ever do to you?" No, Kohl's annoys me all the time, which I'll get to. Moreover, I hate what shopping at Kohl's says about me. It says I have given up, that I have no plans to move to a cosmopolitan city, drink raw pressed juice and buy boxy Japanese blouses at Uniqlo. I am a leggings-wearing, middle-aged white lady with a messy bun in the suburbs who gets the fries refill at Red Robin and shops in person at Kohl's.

Though I may publicly deride the merchandise at Kohl's as uninspired and pedestrian, in truth, Kohl's offers a variety of attractive and practical items at reasonable prices, from cardigan sweaters to shapewear to wet-dry mops. It carries capsule collections from aspirational ladies who probably drink raw pressed juice, like Reese Witherspoon and Lauren Conrad. Also, Kohl's has mini Sephora stores inside now. I'm toast.

And since it's the season, let's not forget that Kohl's has the market cornered on hideous Christmas attire. Kohl's is king of Dad Bar Crawl Chic. If you have ever seen a grown man wearing a three-piece green shorts suit in an alternating ornament and mitten motif, Kohl's has him by the throat. Last year, for an ugly sweater party, I dragged my sad self to Kohl's and purchased a crew-neck sweatshirt featuring holiday cats. The piece de resistance was a button that ... played holiday music in a mewling cat voice. I didn't even discover this button until I got home, at which point I gently wept.

So, yeah, this is who I am, I guess. That hard truth would feel less agitating if Kohl's didn't own me so hard. By this I mean that, via a labyrinth of coupons, store credits and subtle shame,

Kohl's has won the battle of wills. I just know my photo is hanging in a break room of a Kohl's, aging while I spend my libertine late 30s buying sale-rack sweatpants and arguing about my status as a rewards member.

I was just reading about how the Kohl's CEO is stepping down amid falling earnings. This makes no sense. Even in these difficult economic times, my local Kohl's always has long lines of crazed-looking individuals gripping Kohl's Cash, which is the Mark of the Beast.

Then again, maybe customers are burning out on the math, the laborious, multi-step process that is payment. Sure, in theory, one could check out with no coupons. But if you're not that rich, you must open the veins of privacy.

You see, I have given Kohl's my personal information many times, yet proof of my existence remains elusive. We repeat a cycle, me and The System. I enter my phone number, and the cashier says I'm not a member of the dark cabal. I tell her that I spend my waking hours getting texts and emails from Kohl's, as one gets repeated instructional pamphlets from a cult. Eventually, some email address gets me in.

Now, Kohl's Cash. This is the real key to the madness, the secret sauce of retail malaise. As a reward for spending actual money, Kohl's gives you Beast Money. The credit activates days later, though. You want 10 free dollars? You must come back and view more basket-weave throw pillows from the Property Brothers. The Kohl's Cash comes with an attached coupon, and oh my God, I am boring myself.

So, there I was last Friday night, gripping my little coupons. The cashier was lollygagging, so I finally asked if she could ring in my Baphomet Hellfire Kohl's Cash.

"I was waiting to see if you had anything else in your Kohl's Wallet," she said.

"What ... is a Kohl's Wallet?" I asked witheringly, spirit rising up out of my ruined body.

"Oh," she said. "If you're going to be a Kohl's shopper, you really need to have your Kohl's Wallet ready."

I fumbled on my phone, Googling "kohls wallet," and found

some extra coupon. She said, "Yeah, I can take that one." Was it a favor? Is she Don Corleone? I'll never know. She printed out my receipt and handed me a brand-new ticket of Kohl's Cash.

Twenty dollars this time, starting Friday. I will don my cat sweater and wonder if Kohl's is making any real money or just cycling coupons in and out, if I am saving or playing Monopoly, if we are all trapped in a simulation and none of it matters, and if I should just take up residence in the Kohl's housewares department from Black Friday until the end of the holiday season. See you there?

Is This the End of Jeans?

Oct. 8, 2022

I stood in the dressing room staring down a six-button labyrinth, wondering what had happened to jeans as a concept. Had we come this far, and yet, not far at all? Was this 2022? 1992? Or, more accurately, 1942? Were we caught in a denim feedback loop?

You know the button fly I'm talking about. Before the proliferation of zippers, a row of buttons was simply a functional necessity. Still, despite mankind's many technological advances, the fashion Gargamels periodically revert to button-fly jeans as a trend.

Button-fly jeans are a special kind of hell, with tiny, covert crevices sliced into an inch-wide channel of denim. Securing the bottom button is like winning "American Ninja Warrior." The buttons must slide perfectly into the hidden pockets at the exact right angle, chin pressed to chest, shirt all bunched around the armpits, a line of four impatient ladies waiting outside the stall. I am telling you: this is not the kind of manual dexterity test I need at a Red Robin!

So, those were out.

I was in Old Navy, America's most deranged carnival of denim. The sheer variety of jeans in Old Navy is staggering, overwhelming, sometimes disheartening. It's like the designers are trying to see what they can get away with. On this trip, I witnessed a style called Extra High-Rise Balloon Ankle jeans, which look exactly as described.

Are we supposed to look good anymore? What is good? Have I simply conflated the notion of "good" with "skinny" because I was raised by my mother, Paris Hilton? Am I getting hives?

A few months ago, I endeavored to do the impossible: UPDATE MY JEANS STYLE due to societal pressure. I ordered a pair of Old Navy Mid-Rise Boyfriend Straight jeans online. They had a higher waist, a lighter wash and a baggier shape than my geriatric millennial skinny jeans. Because of, I guess, body dysmorphia, I ordered them way too large.

My stepdaughter assured me they were extremely cool. My husband politely suggested I tie a shoestring around the two back belt loops, which... I mean... I haven't worked this hard in life to become someone loping around in strange, pear-shaped, ripped-knee jeans with a shoelace holding up the backside.

However, these giant jeans were comfortable. Really comfortable. More comfortable than any jeans I've ever worn, which is the intent of jeans? They have "boyfriend" in the name, after all, a subliminal signifier of looseness, ease, respite from the shrink-wrapped torture devices many women have squeezed into since the dawn of the sun. Boyfriends: they get to be comfortable and no one else.

The giant boyfriend jeans quickly became a stand-in for sweatpants around the house. I wore them in public on a few occasions, tugging at the waistband the entire time and feeling, well, hideous.

It's hard to welcome anything new when toxic fashion is ingrained in your amygdala. I graduated high school in 2001, a perilous time for jeans. We're talking painted on, shoe-gobbling, too low-rise to sit. It was a sick time to be a girl, really, the tabloid era. The emergence of dark, high-rise skinny jeans in the 2010s felt like a gentle hug for both our self-loathing and lower abdomens.

A looser jeans aesthetic should be a welcome trend for those of us still mentally imprisoned inside a Perez Hilton blog post, no? Why is the journey so loaded?

Last week, I shared a tweet from Carlye Wisel that made me laugh: "Elder millennials: brace yourselves for what's about to come."

Wide-leg, zip-off jeans with cargo pockets! I was SWEATING.

My colleague Christopher Spata chimed in with something I'd never even considered: the idea of giving up.

"This is why I've made the difficult but empowering choice of opting out of jeans," he said. "The garment that is supposed to be the most casual is with each passing cycle more a high-wire act of 'pulling it off'."

He pointed to a 2021 Dave Schilling piece in the Los Angeles Times, positioning denim as a time capsule, a marker of personality and social station. Schilling found Northeast LA residents who won't give up skinny jeans and other "accoutrements of the bygone Obama era."

"Maybe that's why I haven't bothered with jeans in so long," he writes. "They're too tied up in generational angst. The minute I commit to a pair, I've committed to an idea."

That feels true, and because it feels true, it stings. Who are we now? Who am I? After living through a pandemic, after changing nearly everything about my routine and how I live, how do I want to look and dress? Is comfort and practicality more important than a pretense of being alluring? And just who am I luring, anyway? My dog loves me as I am.

Maybe the boyfriend jeans are a form of opting out, in the end. Maybe the younger generation has found a way to express a casual point of view without oversexualizing everything, without sacrificing comfort, without needing three friends to extract them from pants at the night's end.

Yeah! Good theory! Back to Old Navy we go. The boyfriend jeans fit, no shoestring needed. Still comfortable! Still ugly! I added a black and white cropped flannel shirt, because flannels are in style for fall along with their 1990s brethren, cursed button-fly jeans.

I appeared... spoiler alert for the "Dexter" series finale from 2013... I looked like a woodsman. I looked like Dexter after he fakes his death and vanishes to a snowy hill in Oregon. These two items must never be worn together, no matter how much TikTok tells me otherwise.

Still, I liked both pieces separately, so I got them. I will figure it out. And I picked up a pair of Mid-Rise Power Slim Straight jeans, which the sign billed as a cross between a skinny and straight leg. This sign was specifically for me, folks. This sign was for 39-year-olds staring down a vibe shift and looking back wistfully toward Tara Reid, toward a party for Belvedere vodka, toward a swag bag with a Nokia flip phone inside.

Compromise? No time like now. Nix on the button fly, though. On that, I'm standing firm.

Underboob and Floss: Wherefore Art Thou Swimsuits?

Feb. 25, 2023

We sat in the lobby of a swank apartment complex deep into an analysis of a radical Polish vegetarian murder mystery. The glam high rise came with a pool deck full of regulation hotties.

Our book club faced the hottie pool during the discussion of lighthearted romp "Drive Your Plow Over the Bones of the Dead." Between bites of cream cheese and red pepper jelly, we glimpsed a breathtaking vision beyond the glass: The philosophically nonexistent bathing suits of 2023.

One member stared out. Without breaking her gaze, she lifted a broken pita chip to the chesty area where a swimsuit top, in theory, would go.

I mean, good for those women in the chip suits, OK? I sit in admiration and awe. No body shaming, no value judgments, go on with your bad self, be free, et cetera. Still, with spring break around the corner, the phenomenon of disappearing swimwear requires analysis in the same manner as ecofeminist lit.

It's not like miniscule bathing suits are new. Please don't send photos of 1980s thongs; I've seen "Weekend at Bernie's." But in an encouraging step for thin-obsessed mankind, swimwear has become more democratized in the 2020s, marketed and supplied to a wider swath of body shapes. Size inclusivity pays off at the till because, shocker, larger humans also like to swim and look cute.

This beach season's trendiest looks are a feat of engineering, a spiritual challenge for those who want to keep external organs contained. Sports Illustrated summed up runway activity at the latest Miami Swim Week as "microstrappy," and, well, skimpy: "thongs, extreme cutouts, micro tops, underboob cutouts, invisible sides." "Underboob," a phrase last uttered by a stern lady with measuring tape at Victoria's Secret, is now an aesthetic goal for... some people.

This includes Kim Kardashian, seen posing from a variety

of up-angles in the promos for her intimates and swimwear line, Skims. As usual, she outdid everyone by creating a micro thong and top up to size 4X. They went viral on TikTok for providing coverage the size of... yes, tortilla chips. Actually, the set appears to be underwear used as swimsuits, but considering this void of textile, what's the diff?

Teeny bikinis may be part of society's pandemic pendulum swing; remember the predicted Vibe Shift? Meanwhile, Americans are courting an onslaught of retrograde moral panic stoked by power-hungry politicians. My state of Florida, land of swimwear, leads the way in the crackdown on expression. Florida's government is the Ikea Smaland manager telling children not to jump in the ball pit. No fun! No variety! The micro bikini, one could argue, is this millennium's answer to hot pants and miniskirts, a middle finger to didactic manatees.

That said, the pressure. Swimwear trends carry supreme social stress, something women are steeped in every waking second. Make sure your body stays toned, curvy, free of bumps and hair, but don't be shy to show it off! All butts about it!

Where do chip tops leave the proverbial book club? For example, what if your first two-piece bathing suit had full-coverage, high-waisted shorts and a sports halter as high as an Edwardian ruff? What if you are so pale you would catch fire in Skims dental floss? I DON'T KNOW ANYONE LIKE THIS, I AM JUST SPITBALLING.

Or what if, in the words of New York Times writer Jessica Grose, you exist in "the hour between babe and hag." Meaning, you're fleetingly neither too young nor old, enjoying the years when Don Lemon will take you seriously. In this case, swimwear is a tricky dance, and the style options are not glorious. A character in the FX miniseries "Fleishman is in Trouble" nails the Spandex limbo, trudging past pool moms all wearing the same tired tankini. They have given up ab cutouts and underboob, and thusly, given up something unsaid.

It's tempting to get mired in glossy photos, think pieces, TikToks and online shopping, and checking in on reality is vital. So, I popped into Grove Surf & Coffee, a precious store on St. Pete

Beach that sells both divine strawberry matcha lattes and trendy swimwear. Many of the bathing suits, adorable indeed, were the size of youth Band-Aids.

Since I was by the beach, I wandered over. Yes, hotties in loincloths existed, but so did teens in bucket hats and rash guards, retirees in ruffled swim skirts, moms in shorts wrangling strollers, unbothered bohemians wrapped in sea turtle beach towels. People of all shapes, sizes and colors soaked in the sun, dug into the sand and trudged to the car. And no one cared. No one ever cares more than we do inside our own heads.

When it's my turn to host book club, we're going to the beach. I'll bring the chips, but we're eating them.

Finding Joy in a Pair of Robber Baron Shoes

March 19, 2022

I used to dress well, the way an extroverted retiree in Boca dresses well. I've always favored glitter, animal prints, big jewelry, faux fur, highly sculptural hair and anything that resembles a *peignoir.* While I admire chic, minimalist style—for instance, a bare-faced French woman in an olive-green sack dress riding a vintage bike—I have never succeeded in being that woman. I am powerless in the presence of, say, a T-shirt with a whimsical tiger wearing an Elizabethan ruff and horn-rimmed glasses, accompanied by a snappy feminist phrase. Or a baseball cap that says TARPON SPRINGS in all rhinestones. *La mystique feminine!* It is who I am! On this hill I die!

But I lost track of my personal style during the pandemic, went from stomping around an office to being one with the couch. My flippy dresses and crisp jackets metamorphosed into local brewery tank tops, leggings and fear. *La misere.*

Now, life has settled somewhere in the middle. I go to the office a bit and venture out more, but the energy is still crackling on a bad connection. So much has changed in two years, and fashion has left many of us behind. The vibe has shifted. The word "cheugy" became cheugy. My once fun Boca-lady clothes feel outdated and grumpy, like a Judy Greer character in a 2000s romcom. Just dozens of Judy Greers in the form of skinny jeans and *de mode* tops staring at me. *Je suis vide.* I am empty.

And this is how I found myself recently whimpering at the feet of tacky shoes.

We were in the kind of shoe store with rows of boxes and a utilitarian selection of wide sizes. We needed new sneakers for my stepchild. A modest quest, not an indulgent trip.

But *voila!* There they were, bathed in fluorescent big-box light. Cream-colored, iridescent faux snake, ankle strap, wave-stitched rainbow threading, and—*gasp choke die*—plastic gems. The heels were MIRRORS. Do you hear me? The HEELS WERE MIRRORS. I tried them on, knowing they would be foot prison, but they felt pillowy, comfortable, adorable.

Are you watching "The Gilded Age" on HBO? In these shoes, I was Bertha Russell, the new-money wife of 1800s New York City robber baron, George. She is tacky, and, um, representative of modern economic inequality. But if you can get past that, she is fantastic. She dares to drink from cups of *colored glass.* She shows *cleavage.* She arrives *uninvited.* She will plot the demise of everyone around her while wearing *multiple peacock feathers.*

Were the shoes expensive? That's what you want to know. I know it is. I'm not going to give a dollar figure because it doesn't matter. It will mean something different to everyone and lead to EMAILS and @ SIGNS. I was not exactly in a Gucci store. But these pointless shoes cost more than I would normally spend on pointless shoes. I walked away.

I believe my husband spied something flicker in me, the way George Russell oozed pity when Bertha hosted a gala with food for hundreds in her garish manor and no one showed. A tiny flame of tackiness. Maybe a lick of yearning for my old self?

"Throw them on the pile," he said, holding the child's sneakers and some shoes he had chosen for himself that resembled, well, lizard skin. We were all losing it.

"No, you don't have to..."

"LET ME DO SOMETHING NICE FOR MY WIFE," he declared, heroically, proudly, as if wearing a silky cravat and not a Tampa Bay Lightning T-shirt. He was buying out the inventory of the ladies' charity bazaar because those old crones had insulted his wife! He was noble! I swooned!

Now, you are saying, if you are married, don't you share money? Yes, mostly. But shut up, please, that is not the point.

At that moment, we chose ugly shoes. We decided to accept a bit of excess in an age when any sort of unessential joy feels apologetic and wrong. Our shoes, our weird, pointless shoes, were a tiny door leading us back to a place of personality, of color and form, of *joie de vivre.*

No, I have not worn them yet. But when I do, watch out. I will show up uninvited.

Side Parts and Skinny Jeans Are Nice, but Have You Tried Total Irrelevance?

March 6, 2021

It's a rite of passage for any new generation to fight with the one before. Just imagine the ruthless barbs traded between 15th-century serfs over tunic length!

Right now that whole thing is playing out between Gen Z and millennials. Let's review: Millennials were born between 1981 and 1996 and have been blamed for everything since, primarily food in bowls. Gen Z was born after 1996, ready to assume the mantle of misdirected vitriol.

According to Gen Z users on TikTok, there are ways to tell if someone is irreparably old. These include but are not limited to: parting your hair on the side; wearing skinny jeans; using the laugh-cry emoji; sorting yourself into a Harry Potter house; drinking wine; eating avocado toast; and using a fanny pack. Meanwhile, Generation X is somewhere ordering craft bourbon and quitting smoking, fully self-actualized.

Because they have not previously experienced being uncool, millennials are upset. They are retorting, sharing photos to claim the styles of the era, such as platform sandals, patchwork denim and impractically tiny purses. On a related note, I'd like to enter my microscopic Canal Street "Louis Vuitton" cherry-blossom bag from 2002 as evidence, Your Honor.

As an older millennial on the cusp of Gen X—a Xennial, if you will—I have not been cool for some time (Ravenclaw). Compatriots, there is no point in antagonizing the younger set. We are professionals with families and bills and impending existential crises. We had our time. The next generations deserve a chance to wear things they will later regret, too.

There is only one thing left to do: Slip into obsolescence.

No, no, it's not as scary as it sounds. Come, sit down. It's lovely here. What's that over there? It might be a new social media platform, but it's probably just a shadow, or some kind of fire. Don't worry.

Do not learn the new music. Listen to the old stations on the satellite radio that came when you bought the car, letting early Kanye warm you like a blanket. Does Gen Z have satellite radio? Do they drive cars?

Perhaps you are disoriented after finding out an actor you've never heard of has 5 million followers on Instagram. That's because that actor is not for you. No, you do not have to binge the show he is in. You may rewatch "Gossip Girl."

Nor must you post three consecutive photos of yourself in negligibly different poses, with a nonsense caption that says something like, "humpty dumpty" or, "fruit salad." Pick one photo. Caption it: "This is me at the beach. I had a great time, but it was a little cold." Feel the freedom.

Did someone say "yeet" or "simp"? It's fine to ask what it means, but do not start using it yourself. That would be a tragic error you could not come back from.

Here, drink from this chalice. It's full of a wine you love, because you have done the necessary aging to develop your palate. Yes, your habits are questionable, your fashion rooted in the unattainable beauty standards of the early 2000s, your tiny purse full of baggage. But it's your baggage.

I will leave the final word on this matter to our mother, Dionne Warwick, the only person on Twitter worth following:

"Do you think I care what younger generations say about me? I will wear this fanny pack. Who cares."

The Only Vibe Shifts I Will Accept

Feb. 19, 2022

Welcome, class, to zeitgeist competence hour. Today's term is "vibe shift."

"Lady, what?" you say. Vibe shift is the phrase of the moment. It's a trend about trends (!) coined by a trend (!) forecaster and brand consultant named Sean Monahan. He has sliced the last two decades into phases based on fashion, music and politics, predicting what's ahead. Vibe shift is less about the exact shoes we'll wear and more about a sensibility and, well, vibe.

A piece from New York Magazine's The Cut sent the concept viral this week, warning of an impending vibe shift. The story by Allison P. Davis dives deep if you want to spend the afternoon Googling "normcore" and "Red Wing boots" and neighborhoods of Brooklyn.

That's one problem with trend forecasts. There's a world out there full of people who do not live in the cultural epicenters of New York or Los Angeles. Most of us will never party in a Williamsburg warehouse. We might be from, say, Tampa! We might party at Applebee's! We might wear aging plastic flip-flops!

Still, the idea feels right. After years of pandemic fears and restrictions, political division and canceling each other, we're not going back to the way things were. We are burned out, due for a new collective energy. Monahan told The Cut he predicts a move away from stern culture wars, toward the unkempt, party-hearty essence of the early 2000s. I fear for low-rise pants yet celebrate sequined going-out tops.

Look, this is information for cool people. Most of us are not cool. We are going to jobs and school pickup and Target, pondering uses for ground beef on a Tuesday. We are not vibe-shifting until the vibe trickles into that very Target. Personally, I decided to wither on the vine when they tried to take my skinny jeans.

But we *could* use new energy. What, exactly?

Is this the era when we give up the lies? I'm not talking misinformation. I'm talking malls. For instance, cities run red with "food halls," which we can all agree are food courts with a disappointing lack of Sbarro. If the vibe is shifting backward, should we return to suffering malls? While we're at it, should we start using hotels and cable again? Perhaps the new vibe is to admit we've all been had.

Speaking of 24 separate subscription fees, how about a forensic accounting vibe? In the wake of the Great Resignation, the new vibe must include detailed financial explanations, not simply, "I feel happier with less!" I want receipts, QuickBooks spreadsheets, grocery dossiers. I want tutorials on "How To Quit When My Rent Is $4 Trillion and My Landlord Is Miss Hannigan." The accompanying fashion can be green eyeshades and sleeve garters, that's fine.

The early 2000s were fun, except for the ruthless tabloid stuff. A return to kindness and propriety would be lovely. What about a modern Victorian vibe? Let's bring back visiting dresses and feather plumes. Let's speak only of the weather and recent sewing projects. Let's present callers as Lady Fizzlefeld of Hornswoggle Manor. Let us correspond by letter sealed with wax, not via social media. This! This is the only acceptable vibe shift!

It's safer than low-rise jeans, anyway.

10 Simple Questions to Ask Yourself While Getting Dressed

June 26, 2021

Recently, I got dressed to ... wait for it ... leave the house and meet someone. It was a casual, professional thing, nothing to dress up for. But, clothes! I have so many, and yet I wear the same three stretchy outfits every week working from home.

I changed three times, settling on jeans and a sparkly, shiny, silver tank top thing with a tie waist. I thought it was festive yet laid back.

"You're wearing your 'going out' top," my husband said. If you lived through the early 2000s, you know exactly what this is. It's a Paris Hilton-adjacent spangled shirt one pairs with jeans for a night on the town, possibly satin, maybe beaded, perchance halter.

I realized it was the middle of the afternoon, probably a little early for glitter. I had no time to change. I had to accept that, while I was once a stylish person, I had forgotten how to dress.

After I posted my sparkle look on Instagram stories, folks replied that they no longer present well in society, either. One tried to wear sequins to an early dinner, and her partner stopped her. "I feel lucky to have a check on my drama as I leave the house," she said.

It's a combination of things, I think. There's the lack of socializing. Folks stopped going to offices. A lot of frontline workers wear uniforms. We are out of practice.

But also ... didn't styles change, like, a lot? Am I imagining it? Surely fashion is always evolving, but the millennial/Gen Z divide with jeans and side parts and the word "cheugy" really came down hard this year. The combo of factors has left a populace disoriented and dressing like we are in "The Big Lebowski."

For help, I have formulated a list of questions one should ask oneself after getting dressed, but before leaving the house:

No. 1. What time is it? Is it noon? 5 p.m.? 2 a.m.? Have I

slipped through an interdimensional portal where time ceases to be?

No. 2. What type of event am I attending? Client meeting? Date? Tarts and vicars party? Family reunion? Building homes? Learning to windsurf? Receiving an Academy Award?

No. 3. Will I be sweating, and how much?

No. 4. Is there potential to run into anyone I haven't seen in 12 to 15 years?

No. 5. Do I like this outfit, or am I wearing it because I feel bad for it? Am I projecting emotional hang-ups on inanimate objects again?

No. 6. Is this clothing going to distract me all night, in the manner of a shoe that makes a little gas-passing noise every time I step?

No. 7. Can I move freely, or will I stand in the corner smiling with top and bottom teeth like Chandler Bing?

No. 8. Did I forget that this shirt has a mustard stain?

No. 9. Does this belong to me, or did I borrow this from the friend I am visiting? Will she remember, or is she just as lost?

No. 10. Am I still cool? Follow up: Do I care?

Tom Brady Washed Up At 45? Welcome to the Life of a Woman.

Jan. 21, 2023

When the Tampa Bay Buccaneers' season came tumbling down Monday night, hot takes about old Tom Brady started flying. And I do mean old.

Everyone was making fun of his age, a decrepit, dusty 45. Get back in the crypt, Tom! A New York Magazine headline read: "Tom Brady Is a Rickety Old Man Still Chasing the Dragon." Shazam! Tampa Bay Times columnist John Romano opined that Tom should look into the AARP app.

After snorting out some Diet Coke, I felt a little bad for Tom. Yeah, comments about his age come relative to the sport of football, not his usefulness on Earth. And 45 is hardly elderly. He can take myriad more drunken boat rides around Tampa Bay, should he desire.

Then, a little gremlin voice rose from my temporal lobe sounding like Edna Mode. She said, "HISS. WHY DO YOU FEEL BAD, LADY? FIE ON TOM. FIE ON THE MEN. MAY THEY SUFFER. MAY THEY RETURN TO DUST." The gremlin reminded me what it's like to exist as a woman getting older. Haha! Welcome to hell, Tommy!

You see, advertisements, movies, tabloids and social media inform women repeatedly and in perpetuity that our youth, desirability and value will dry up at an early age. We will stop being hot and fresh around... oh, 14? Or so? That's when our faces begin to crease from expressing emotion, a big no-no. The standard of beauty in the West is a blonde, white-but-tan, oiled porpoise with no body hair. She smells like a strawberry jellybean, has lips like pontoons, eyelashes in the chrysalis stage of the caterpillar life cycle.

We must achieve this proximity at all co$t. Have you watched a woman contouring her face? Do you know the difference between liquid and powder blush, universal C skin refiner and microencapsulated retinol? Do you know how much a high-quality tube of concealer costs so that we may most effectively hide our hideous natural countenance? You know who probably knows this? Gisele probably knows this!

Do you know how we keep our nails looking fresh, young and healthy? We dip them in a combination of ETHYL CYANOACRYLATE and POLYMETHYL METHACRYLATE for $50 every three weeks.

Do you know about hair extensions? Microblading? Electrolysis? Have you heard of a *butt mask*? A microcurrent device? Do you know we are hiding in our bathrooms sending low-voltage electrical currents into facial muscles to achieve "snatched jawlines"?

Do you know about Restylane, Botox, Dysport, Xeomin, Belotero, Volbella, Voluma, Kybella? Do you know my friend sent me photographs of her red, puffy injection points last week, and we had a heart to heart, made a pact to let our faces turn into whatever our faces turn into?

Has Tom Brady had buccal fat pad removal? This is a serious question, because his cheekbones are popping.

Furthermore, you must know, women's *body types are trends.* For instance, the Brazilian Booty Lift aesthetic is out. It is fashionable to look hungry, as if constantly sucking a lozenge. In addition, we must deploy photo filters with utmost care. We shall appear young and effervescent, but not too young and effervescent, else the internet will roundly mock us in the manner of Madonna and Paula Abdul.

Women can no longer date Leonardo DiCaprio past 25; this is canon. But let's turn to Nicole Kidman for further analysis of midlife in Hollyweird, the laboratory for all arbitrary gender rules. In 2021, she said: "There's a consensus in the industry that as a female actor, at about 40, you're done." While men can flourish as salt-and-pepper daddies, female love interests are often decades junior to leading men. Women over 40 are more likely to be cast as a psychotic school headmistress with a penchant for shot put (see: Emma Thompson in "Matilda." Inspired performance).

We already know having children causes career

interruption. The pandemic worsened working conditions for women of a certain age, many of whom were trying to teach their children to reduce fractions while balancing a laptop atop a pile of KN95 masks. An AARP study (did you get your card, Tom?) found midcareer and older women suffered outsized job interruption since 2020, with Black and Hispanic women topping that list.

And since we're talking about football, no one ever seems to discuss the plight of athletes with periods, or who carry and deliver actual human beings. What about their changing bodies? Their perimenopause, fluctuating hormones, hot flashes, sweating, muscle aches? Do you know about the benefits of hyaluronic acid applied via jade ice rollers???

Serena Williams, who was two months pregnant when she won the Australian Open in 2017 (!!), retired from tennis last year at 40. She wrote this in Vogue: "If I were a guy, I wouldn't be writing this because I'd be out there playing and winning while my wife was doing the physical labor of expanding our family. Maybe I'd be more of a Tom Brady if I had that opportunity."

We don't know what creaky, fossilized, enfeebled Tom will do next, though he will likely announce his decisions just past deadline on a Friday night, because that is his vibe. But it's fair to say that once he steps off the field, he will be allowed to age gracefully, with his fine lines and gray hairs blazing on television as long as he chooses, never needing to know what a butt mask is. So, he can take a few more hits.

Be Cultured

Did Millennials or Gen X Drink Water Growing Up? An Investigation.

March 7, 2023

When I reflect on my childhood in the context of beverages, I primarily remember two things: Kool-Aid and Tang.

These 1980s staples were not the portrait of "wellness," a cursed word we'll explore more momentarily. But they were my drinks. I was lactose intolerant as a child (this is off to a cool, sexy start) so I had juice most of the time with meals. My brother and I had free rein to pick heaps of little Kool-Aid powder packets in exciting different flavors. I think they were 10 cents or a quarter back then. We mixed up monstrous servings in a brown plastic pitcher that lived in the refrigerator until it was depleted and ready for more. I do believe there was—shudder—a cup of white sugar involved, but maybe spread over 12 glasses, that's not so bad? I don't know, it's probably bad.

There was water IN the Kool-Aid, of course. But the thing that has been haunting me lately is that I can't remember drinking just plain water. I have no memories of going to the sink and filling a glass, then kicking back and consuming that killer H2O. I certainly didn't carry a water bottle to school. These days, some schools require it; our middle schooler carries one daily. To be honest, I don't know if I even owned a refillable water bottle until my 20s.

I mean, look, I'm sure I did drink water! My parents are probably reading this insisting that I drank water, cursing as I smear their good name. They took excellent care of us and fed us vegetables. I am alive, am I not? (No, really, am I?) But millennial and Gen X kids were simply not raised with today's hydration fetish.

I surveyed peers in this age bracket on Instagram. Few reported drinking water either. Some answers: Crystal Light, Capri Sun, milk, apple juice, Hi-C, Five Alive, Hawaiian Punch, Sunny Delight, Snapple and soda (or pop, depending on the part of the country you're from). Several reminisced about being marched to the drinking fountain in a single-file line after recess, at which point we would all put our mouths on the same spigot while the teacher counted to three with the word "Mississippi" and told us to save some for the fishes. In 2023, can you even fathom?

Water usage, based on my ironclad anecdotal survey, began trending up in our college era. This marks the debut of individual plastic bottles, the scourge of the environment, as well as Brita water filtration pitchers. These babies lived in countless university apartments, each roommate avoiding the responsibility of the refill.

This trajectory matches the actual reporting. American water consumption rose with both the proliferation of bottled water and the marketing of water as an overall tool of "wellness." This, we know, is a toothless term that implies a mystical, pricey fix for every ailment (looking at you, Goop). Of course, I'm not saying water is a scam. I should drink more water! I am turning to dust as I type!

But we probably don't need as much as we think, the same way we don't really need 10,000 steps per day. In 2020, a kidney specialist at the University of Virginia told The New York Times that desk jockeys needn't guzzle water like athletes, who are the basis for most studies, and that if we overhydrate, we potentially just pee out sodium and electrolytes. A 2015 study found that milk and orange juice actually did a better job of hydration than water (fist pump to all the millennial kids eating green beans and milk, hork!). You'll probably not see milk and OJ getting the same marketing traction these days because they have calories and America is fatphobic.

Since we know disposable plastic bottles Are Not It, the sales pitch has shifted to reusable bottles, each new brand guaranteed to make us crusty, dehydrated Sunny D kids finally glow from within. The Stanley, the Hydro Flask, the S'well, the Yeti. These are as much status symbols as hydration tools. Per market researchers at The NPD Group, U.S. consumers spent $3.3 billion on portable drink bottles midway through 2022, 20% more than the year before.

Why am I floating down this river of pain? BORGS, that's why. BORGS are... well, there's no getting around it. BORG stands for blackout rage gallon. This trend has been on college campuses for some time now, but all us olds recently caught on after seeing TikToks, so the articles are flying. Basically, a BORG is a gallon water jug sans half the water and mixed with alcohol, flavor drops and electrolyte powder like Liquid I.V. Students cap the jugs and write funny names on them, like "Ruth Bader Ginsborg."

Disclaimer that I am not out here advocating for binge drinking in this manner! It is a bad idea at any time of life to consume half a bottle of vodka. Some chill older folks, like, you know, English professor aunts who let you crash at their lake condos and don't tell your mom, claim the wee adults are actually practicing harm reduction with BORGs due to the measuring, water and electrolytes. Plus, the jugs are capped, labeled and kept near, reducing the chance for anyone to slip in drugs. Hard to argue.

However, I will never be able to vouch if a BORG minimizes hangovers or harm, because I do think that drinking one at this age might literally kill me. I also never drank punch out of bathtub in college, as many in my peer group are pointing out. Though, there was one time where we tried to make "sangria" for Halloween and dumped Carlo Rossi into a plastic witch cauldron from Party City along with A CONTAINER OF CANTALOUPE AND WATERMELON. I don't want to talk about it.

Basically, I'm just saying, the youth are all about hitting their hydration goals, even when perched on the hood of a Prius twerking outside Delta Delta Delta, whereas I can't remember a single time in my younger days when I ever sat down with a nice cup of hydrogen and oxygen in a liquid state. I am simultaneously impressed, skeptical, jealous, concerned, admiring and curious. But mostly, I am thirsty.

The Guilt Spiral of Tipping in 2023

May 13, 2023

Much goes unsaid between customers and workers, an icy chasm between "We have Pepsi products; is that OK?" and "Get home safe!" Therein writhes a silent disco of pain, I am telling you.

You see, America decided to let people pay each other on a system of vibes and vibes alone. We really said, "Strangers shall make wage assessments over a $14 panini, deciding which party will afford electricity that week. Both parties will be wildly self-conscious and full of guilt. They will Charlie Brown-stare each other to death while smiling through gritted teeth until everyone ends up broke and miserable. Cosigned, John Hancock and the rest."

Of course, we are talking about tipping. The service-based gratuity is a storied tradition that has become more unbridled than ever. Americans are no longer expected to just tip on dinners (no, Pepsi is not OK), haircuts and car rides. The popularity of fingerprinty iPads at checkout counters, coupled with the financial trauma of the pandemic, has turned life into a Drake video in which we're all giving each other nickels while corporate overlords spread baby oil on their bellies. We not only tip servers, whose baseline pay is the last dime Grandpa Joe gave Charlie Bucket. We tip everyone, and a lot, unless we don't, but maybe we should, unless we shouldn't, please help?

New York Magazine decided to swing big and set new rules for tipping: While it was once socially acceptable to tip 15 to 20%, 20% is the new minimum for dining. The magazine advised 20% at coffee shops, too, and $5 or 20% minimum on food delivery. And yes, we're supposed to leave $1 on a bottle of water when the cashier swivels around that cursed iPad and says, "Just a couple questions." Meanwhile, the Los Angeles Times recently outlined tipping's racist and classist roots, history always a rat in the floorboards.

I did not come here today to talk about solutions, however, because no one likes those, either. I came here for psychological commiseration. If you are like me, by which I mean, "raised going to confession," let's talk. Tipping introduces a frequent opportunity for a Cirque du Moo-lah acrobatic show of guilt, indignation, empathy and ultimately, exhaustion.

For example, can this barista see where my finger is trailing? Does she know the $1 option is on the left? Does she know I'm a good person? Why do I care if she likes me? I want her to like me.

Do I tip on this jar of artisanal artichokes? I took it off the shelf myself, so no one really did anything. There are 16 people behind me in line, and they can all sense I'm deciding whether to tip and judging me for it in six different ways. If I wedge in a supportive comment about collective bargaining, can I skip the tip? Oh my God, did I just wink?

I am in self-checkout. Am I tipping a robot? Does the robot like me?

Did UberEats increase one-click tipping to 16% and 21%? Are they really going to make me do math at a time like this, a time when I am sans tacos?

What is 20% of eleventy billion dollars? That will cover the tip on these beers someone pulled out of a pool of gray ice water at a stadium. He seems nice. It's not his fault.

Yes, my soup was full of hair and staples, but it's not like the server put the hair and staples in the soup, right? I can't punish everyone. Plus, the server splits tip with the back of house and the host, a fact I know from my time working as a host—those little envelopes filled with $20 of tip share pay for gas to get back to the restaurant to get more little $20 envelopes to pay for more gas to get back to the restaurant. Hmm, maybe by not tipping, I am liberating the host from this toxic cycle! Maybe that is the moral choice? No. I'll tip $400, because that is the social contract. I'll eat the hair and staples.

Literally everyone hates me.

Requiem for Bed Bath & Beyond

May 6, 2023

Goodbye to Bed Bath & Beyond.

Goodbye to yet another American corporate comfort that just couldn't hang, filing for bankruptcy protection and falling to rest near brethren Toys "R" Us, Tuesday Morning, Stein Mart and Sports Authority. Goodbye to a big-box retail wonderland woefully behind the times, lost to the couch-surfing ease of internet shopping. And yet, goodbye to something, somehow, timeless.

Goodbye to the stacks of invasive blue coupons refusing to be ignored, clogging the mailbox, sticking out of chaotic kitchen drawers, dangling from countless refrigerators via local pizza shop magnets.

Goodbye to hectic parking lots, to automatic doors, to rushes of icy air conditioning, to fluorescent lights and cavernous warehouse ceilings. Goodbye to soft favorites playing gently overhead. Goodbye to "Unbreak My Heart."

Goodbye to epic posters of beautiful humans living their best lifestyles. A man, barefoot atop a burlap rug, holding an adorable infant staring at a bowl of brown eggs. A woman in a white bathrobe perched on the edge of a bathtub, hair in a chignon, setting the water temperature just so. A blissful couple gleefully chopping rainbow chard to accompany their pristine quiche.

Goodbye to the real couples wandering the store with a wedding registry device, scanning housewares they never knew they needed until confronted with the possibility of limitless gifts. Artfully mismatched Fiestaware. J.A. Henckels knife sets. Gold-plated utensils with service for 12 friends they may or may not have.

Goodbye to the Bed and the Bath, yes, but goodbye mostly to the smorgasbord of wonderful, weird, wild Beyond. Sure, buy these items online if you must, but feel no joy of random discovery.

Goodbye to the TravelJohn, a resealable, disposable urinal perfect for road trips, camping, boating and more. Leakproof! Hygienic!

Goodbye to Herb & Lou's infused ice cube cocktail mixers in pink grapefruit paloma with cinnamon, basil and chilies. Goodbye to the promise of elegance, sucker.

Goodbye to the most SodaStream content anyone has ever seen.

Goodbye to a $400 Homedics kinetic sand table with a little ball that rakes a hypnotic pattern in the powder. Goodbye, mindfulness!

Goodbye to coasters and mugs with so much to say: RAD DAD. MY HEART IS IN THE U.S.A. TROPICAL VIBES. SWEATER WEATHER. LOVE IS BREWING.

Goodbye to UGG brand classic sherpa pet hats and coordinating socks, a great gift set for the fashionable yet chilly animal companion in your life.

Goodbye to digital scales featuring smiling women on the box hugging their knees beside a dysmorphic reading of, always, 127.2 pounds. That one can go, actually.

Goodbye to the checkout lines filled with impulse items, sour candies, face mask holders, bottle brushes, As Seen On TV garage door motion lights, all begging you to give them one more look.

Goodbye to the frantic, last-minute search through your phone for a text or email coupon, because despite having so many billboard-style savings vouchers infiltrating your home, you never remember to actually bring them to the store. It doesn't matter anyway, you realize upon reading a sad, printed sign at the register. The coupons are over.

It's all over.

Hello to the tiny glass butter dish that charmed you on your last lap through the liquidating store. It was $8. You're not sure why you had to have it, but you did. It's a little reminder of a familiar American era of browsing and bargains, maybe, a retail ritual disappearing a bit more each year.

Final sale.

Let Swifties Have Their Joy!

April 8, 2023

They say comparison is the thief of joy, but you know what else is a thief of joy? Thieves of joy!

Joy thievery is an occupation, a volunteer-based paramilitary calling with many dedicated adherents. Everyone has met a Joy Thief, one who believes so strongly in their own cultural correctitude, their own precious coolness that they expend exorbitant words, just so many words, pointing out that mainstream tastes are stupid, pointless and worthy of ridicule.

If you have not met a person like this, well, hold on...

(writer pauses to retrieve tiny, bejeweled mirror from an overpriced concert tote bag, holds it up)

There.

Joy Thieves can be found on first dates monopolizing the conversation with details about their tour of foreign eco-hostels mere moments after you say you really love living in your hometown. They will tell you about the sodium nitrite levels in your cheeseburger as said cheeseburger is entering your mouth. Their love language is sarcasm, their superpower, capital letters. Favorite phrases include "ACTUALLY" and "WHO CARES." They can be found in the comments section once this column is posted on Facebook.

A Joy Thief cannot simply register something that doesn't personally interest them and head on down the old, dusty trail. No, a Joy Thief must step in to correct their victim. This is different from, say, a critic who dissects art in a thoughtful, contextual way or an activist who calls out actual wrongdoing. A Joy Thief exists solely to be a huge bummer. A Joy Thief just wants you to know your music is bad!

Now, why are we talking about this? Because Taylor Swift is making her way around the country, thrilling audiences on her Eras tour. She will perform three concerts in my town of Tampa in a matter of days, her only stop in Florida. These concerts constitute regional news in the tenor of "major weather event" or

"Super Bowl," like it or not.

Yes, I am going! Yes, I spent a lot of money on a ticket! No, I do not consider Taylor Swift a guilty pleasure. I consider her one of the best songwriters Of Our Time and I will gladly sit over a glass of a Joy Thief's favorite organic, sulfite-free wine and annotate the narrative arc of the teenage love triangle presented on the "Folklore" album.

Perhaps I am a little salty. My Lavender Hayes-themed concert dress (see what I did there?) showed up days ago and was the ugliest thing on the planet. I looked like I was assaulted by the Easter Bunny. I looked like a smashed Jordan almond from a bridal shower when all I wanted was to belly flop into the glee of crowd participation. I have gone back to the drawing board, sartorially speaking, so I am...

(writer pauses to find retail receipt)

...on edge.

Here's what I am saying, though. These days, in this world, it's a challenge to love anything. Like, it's hard to buy toothpaste without knowing if the pharmacy chain has committed human rights violations. It is impossible to watch a stand-up special without scanning the "personal life" section of Wikipedia for atrocities. Around 2017, I started saying "Love nothing, trust no one" each time I opened a website.

To be enthusiastic anymore somehow feels pure, silly, fragile. One of the many reasons Swift's fans adore her is because she embraces the joyful, goofy side of the fandom: the friendship bracelets, the Easter eggs in her posts, the unhinged fan theories. She supports fans dressing up like her cats, named for characters on a Joy Thief's least-favorite shows, "Law & Order: Special Victim's Unit" and "Grey's Anatomy."

Swifties are a little intense, yes, but that's because they are backed by Swift herself, who once uttered these wise words: "The worst kind of person is someone who makes someone feel bad, dumb or stupid for being excited about something."

Indeed! Next time a guy drinking a session IPA (fine to like IPAs, though!) calls your interest basic, overplayed, whatever, tell him he is wrong. Present the following list of things that are also fine for people to love until further notice. He will hate it:

Compact discs, Minions, "The Big Bang Theory," Red Lobster, comic cons, "The Bachelor," Pitbull, Starbucks, Kohl's, Dave Matthews Band, "The Office," Bitmoji, Diet Coke, "Bel-Air," Taco Bell, romance novels, astrology, mall pretzels, Target, scented candles, professional wrestling, Zumba, "Emily in Paris," Domino's pizza, Halloween and, reluctantly, Crocs.

Carry on with the business of shameless love, the perfect bedazzled shoes, the lyrics in your head rolling off your tongue. Feel the kin around you, understanding, forming a memory in real time. In the big picture, what a small pleasure it is to be a fan.

Goat Yoga and More Things I'm Deinfluencing

Feb. 18, 2023

Have you heard about the trend of deinfluencing?

First, let's assume you know about influencing. People with online audiences recommend products, vacations, restaurants and anything con$umable, sometimes for money or gifts. Yes, I am describing advertising, but the vibes are different when social media enters the fray. A social influencer is someone we like to follow, who has gained our trust and whose recommendations we take seriously.

I'm a perfect mark! A late-30s woman with a little disposable income, plugged into the internet while simultaneously confronted with the woeful realities of aging. I'm doomed. Just ask the too-long flare yoga pants in my closet I keep threatening to hem. Ask the neutral boho top that looked cool on the influencer but like a literal bowl of Quaker instant oats on me. Ask the strawberry kefir chia pudding in my fridge. Ask the 68-pound Revlon drying brush I've used three times in three years. Ask my Rare Beauty cream blush, a current influencer staple, which I actually like very much. ASK MY PILLOW SLIDES.

However, this blind susceptibility to commerce is not sustainable. Why do I need four different lip glosses in the same shade of nude? Why do I believe every new hair tool will give me a transformed head? Enter deinfluencing, the practice of TikTokers sharing viral products they actually don't like. Here's a bit from Time:

"The growing trend is a direct response to the endless deluge of products that beauty and lifestyle influencers insist you simply must have. According to the internet, at the moment, you should own a Stanley Cup drink tumbler, an ice roller for your face, shapewear from Kim Kardahian's SKIMS line and some tinned fish in your kitchen cupboard. These are subject to change next month, or next week—depending on trends."

Brands must be quaking a little, and I like this. I like it a lot.

I think we can extend this practice well beyond beauty and lifestyle products. Plenty of life experiences also need deinfluencing.

For starters, I would like to deinfluence funny animal yoga.

Have you ever done goat yoga? It is exactly like it sounds: yoga in the presence of goats. I did it in Nashville and can boldly say that it was the stupidest thing I've ever attempted. Goat flow might have been more idyllic in a pasture, but this was a glorified garage with the door rolled up for airflow. The goats peed and pooped all over our yoga mats. Getting into actual yoga positions or a flowy state of mind was impossible because, as mentioned, GOATS WERE DEFECATING ON US. The goats did not want to be there. The people, by the end, did not want to be there. This was not about yoga, nor goats. This was about a photo op, and yes, I did get mine. It was not worth it.

Speaking of photo ops, let's deinfluence whimsical neon signs, which will soon be a dreadful remnant of 2020s urban center monoculture. I am done posing in a tapas restaurant bathroom under pink tube lighting that spells "YOU GLOW GIRL." I am done pretending I just happened to take a candid photo under an effulgent blue cafe sign that says, "BUT FIRST COFFEE." Yes, there should be a comma in both of these expressions, but neon signs never have correct punctuation!

While we're at it, let's deinfluence day-in-the-life-videos. I don't believe for a second that someone set up her phone on a tripod and let it roll all night so she could hop out of bed in full makeup and yawn cutely at the true hour of her waking. She recreated that! Which is fine, just say it! How do influencers with kids do this? Do they set the camera up just to corral the kids into shoes and the car, only to go back into the house with the children, take the camera down and usher the kids back in the car? Or do they leave the kids in the car while they dismantle the filming materials?

I guess let's just deinfluence doing things just for the sake of the photo. Photos are great, witnessing little insights into a mundane day. There's real connection in that. But there has to be a more abiding reason for participating in an activity other than just the photo, right? There has to be a reason to buy the Stanley tumbler other than the fact that everyone else has the Stanley tumbler. Next time we make plans, let us ask ourselves: If my phone fell into a burning ring of fire and no one on Earth knew what I was up to, would I still go to goat yoga? I think I know the answer.

Incredibly, the Queen's Funeral Is Still Going On: An Explainer

Sept. 17, 2022

Understanding Queen Elizabeth II's historic funeral is a full-time job, one I have selflessly devoted myself to undertaking. Editors, please accept my resignation for the other stuff.
Someone has to sort through the cognitive dissonance. Why does the queen's coffin linger on television so long after her death, rolling past cursed chyrons that read MYPILLOW CEO MIKE LINDELL SERVED WITH SUBPOENA AT HARDEE'S?

I am not here to disrespect Her Majesty, who was dedicated to her nation. Like many heterosexual, white women, I've been a casual royals watcher since Prince William appeared on the cover of YM magazine in 1998 as "PRINCE OF OUR HEARTS." I'm also not here to dismiss the colonizing, musty, problematic nature of the monarchy. We in the States know all about colonizing, musty problems.

Nay, I am merely here for what we in journalism call an "explainer," or alternately, an excuse to use bullet points:

— The queen died in Scotland on Sept. 8, setting in motion Operation Unicorn, a supporting plan to Operation London Bridge. This preparedness makes sense to me. The plans involved the Church of England, the Metropolitan Police Service, the British Armed Forces, the media and many others. I have six Google docs just to visit Universal Studios in Orlando.

— Charles became king under Operation Spring Tide. Again, I will not comment. I will strain-smile into my lap and struggle to make meaningful eye contact. A council of important people said, yeah, he's king. Charles proclaimed that, yeah, I'm king, then signed a paper that, yeah, I'm king. "How nice for Charles," I said before sliding on my Princess Diana commemorative ring from Michaels arts and crafts.

— The queen's coffin moved to Balmoral Castle on Sept. 9. Two days later, it moved to the Palace of Holyroodhouse, which I can't believe is a real place. From there, it went to St. Giles'

Cathedral in Edinburgh, then Buckingham Palace in London.

— The Daily Mail reported that the "royal beekeeper informed the Queen's bees that the Queen has died and King Charles is their new boss." Privately, several senior royals wondered why the monarchy isn't taken more seriously.

— People Magazine hammered breaking news alerts that the embattled Will, Kate, Harry and Meghan took a walk together in a show of solidarity. Yes, this funeral involves actual archers and a crown crusted in an unspeakable wealth of diamonds, but no. This. This, to me, was the most wildly royal moment. The simple act of walking while issuing icy sidelong glares.

— The Royal Parks asked mourners to stop leaving Paddington bears and marmalade sandwiches at memorials. The jamwiches do seem like an ant trap, but banning Paddington is heretical at best.

— News coverage has been exhaustive. Wall-to-wall. Harry Styles-level overexposed. Just after 4 p.m. on Wednesday, CNN aired a story titled "Leaking Pen Frustrates King Charles: 'This Bloody Thing.''" In a very real segment, a leaking pen frustrated King Charles.

— A ceremonial procession brought the coffin to Westminster Hall, where the queen lies in state. This reminds me of when Hal from Moss Feaster Funeral Home sticks a light on top of a Plymouth Sundance and all us Catholics cruise past the Ace Hardware. In this case, Hal is the King's Troop Royal Horse Artillery and is *(murmurs)* probably not Catholic.

— We got a glimpse of Princess Anne, who is an offensive 16th in line for the throne. Can you believe this? In 2011—which the court would remind you is not very long ago—the monarchy decided women could finally be equal to their nasty brothers. But not Anne, one of the busiest royals, because she was born in the old days. Paddington would like a word with the manager.

— Speaking of brothers, alleged sexual predator and Epstein cohort Prince Andrew got permission to wear his military uniform at the last vigil, but Harry did not, when all Harry wants to do is podcast with Megs in Cali.

— Well-wishers have been lining up to pay respects in

"The Queue," temporarily shut down Friday when it reached five miles. Sources say British people really like to stand in line. Many were somber, separating queasy feelings for the monarchy from their love of the woman. The New York Times spotted gin and tonic in line, which I think the queen would cosign? She notoriously cherished gin, buoying data for those of us who also cherish gin and aspire to be 96.

— Monday marks her OFFICIAL official funeral, at which point People is going to make my inbox a shambles. The queen will then go to her final resting place, St. George's Chapel at Windsor Castle. She will join her husband Prince Philip, her sister and her parents. Television news will, as a concept, pass out from dehydration. Some of us will go back to searching through old bins for that magazine with William.

— I would like my other job back now. Please?

Watching The Sopranos Is Relaxing. Am I Broken?

Oct. 2, 2021

As Tony Soprano knocked out a guy's teeth for talking to his daughter, I clutched my warm mug of tea. The cinnamon steam wafted into my nose. So mellow, like a spa day!

It's my second viewing of "The Sopranos." This time, I'm picking off episodes while reading a companion guide called "The Sopranos Sessions," which is voluminous enough to be a mob weapon. The show is a parade of murderous, misogynistic, bigoted characters who are somehow still, I don't know, funsies. Watching them is the best part of my day.

"The Sopranos" is also an art piece, a time capsule of declining civilization and a prototype for antihero television. But this isn't about why the show is good. With "The Many Saints of Newark" prequel movie out now, there are hundreds, nay, thousands, nay, *millions* of takes about the show's legacy.

I'm just wondering what's wrong with me. I make my living trying to find humor and joy in life. I spend a lot of time writing jokes. I am generally pleasant!

Then, before bed, I unwind with beheadings on "Game of Thrones"; meth-making on "Breaking Bad"; street killings on "The Wire"; demonic babies on "American Horror Story"; and functional alcoholism on "Mare of Easttown."

Once a week, on Macabre Monday, my husband and I watch a horror movie. This week, we watched "Saint Maud," a film about a devoutly religious woman who gets more and more extreme. I won't spoil the ending, but it's brilliant. And absolutely horrific.

"Ready for bed?" I said during the credits.

"After THAT?" he said, and turned on "The Office."

Yes, millions of people are still watching "The Office" during the eternal pandemic. Viewers also watched 30.5 billion minutes of "Ozark," a show about a money-laundering dad, and 19 billion minutes of "Lucifer," a show about, um, the devil.

I called Dawn Cecil to diagnose my issues. The University of South Florida professor studies media representations of crime and justice and teaches a class on crime media and pop culture. Her book "Fear, Justice and Modern True Crime" examines the rapid growth of true-crime TV and podcasts.

"What I do ruins what I watch sometimes," she said.

Cecil watched "The Sopranos" when it came out, with no academic strings attached, marveling at how it twisted expectations for television. Later, she got into the "Serial" podcast and began breaking down human attraction to gritty stories.

I posited that they tap into our cultural anxieties and give us tools to grapple with them. They offer conflict, which we have in spades, and resolution, which we are sorely lacking.

There's no single reason people flock to darkness, Cecil said. The complex storylines can stimulate our brains. They can be therapeutic for people who've lived through trauma. They can be purely escapist.

"Like, my life is not so bad after all," she said. "People have it so much worse."

And maybe, Cecil has learned, we don't have to work so hard to defend it. Maybe it's OK to like what we like.

So, if you're with me, clear your calendar for that new cult docuseries. Listen to medical malpractice podcasts on the treadmill. Politely thank friends who recommend a sitcom, then ignore them. Keep on doing what moves you, like Tony Soprano staring at ducks in his swimming pool.

How to Discuss Daylight Saving Time (No S!) Like You Understand It

Nov. 6, 2021

We all know it's time to "fall back," or set clocks an hour earlier Sunday. This is an old-fashioned way of saying "relax while your Apple products automatically reset."

We know the implications, too. It means our babies, dogs, parakeets and lawn mowers will start screeching earlier. Our evening walks will be in the dark. It will take days, nay, weeks for our bodies to adjust, all while fighting off seasonal affective disorder. This, conveniently, coincides with the holiday season, which is not a stressful time at all!

There's the basic information. But are you fine knowing the bare minimum? I thought so. I will tell you more anyway.

The first thing to know is that daylight savings time is actually daylight SAVING time, with no extra "S." You should obnoxiously correct anyone who says it incorrectly, which is everyone.

How do I know? It happened to me. And once someone is obnoxious to you, it is your civic duty to pay it forward. It's how you drive through Starbucks and a person has paid for your drink, and now you have to *&^&$#@ do it, too, except the person behind you spent $34 on breakfast sandwiches and seasonal drinks, and you just ordered a tea.

We're not going to be in daylight saving time; we are leaving it and going back to "standard time," which runs through March and is less sexy. Research shows people reply to standard time party invites with, "We have another thing, but maybe we'll swing by!"

Efforts to end standard time have lumbered along in many states. I will quote Tampa Bay Times reader R.O. Plummer of Palm Harbor, Florida, who recently asked: "When is Sen. Marco Rubio going to put a stop to that? He says he's working on it. How difficult could it be?"

I don't know. It seems difficult, but that's why I am not a

senator (also the long hours, suits, moral compromises). It requires an act of Congress. I personally believe Congress does not want to give up the mental image of Rubio angrily winding a grandfather clock, holding a lantern and wearing a long, woolen sleeping cap.

Instead of looking for solutions, let's look for someone to blame.

Travel to 1918, another awful pandemic year. The U.S. copied Europe and introduced daylight saving time to save coal during World War I. We didn't use the time change again until the next war. So, we must blame Franklin D. Roosevelt, and war.

Why can't states just do what they want? That's the American vibe. Well, an act from 1966 lets states and territories permanently opt OUT of daylight saving time but not IN. Do you follow? Neither do I. Ask Hawaii, Arizona, Puerto Rico, Guam, the Virgin Islands, American Samoa and the Northern Marianas Islands, 'cause they have figured it out.

Civilizations have messed with clocks since the dawn of industry, usually to squeeze more work out of people. And getting rid of standard time won't solve all our problems. It would make winter mornings really dark; consider school safety, traffic accidents, how our hair looks.

I expect passionate letters on both sides, like when I recently wrote that candy corn is gross. But maybe we need to ask ourselves, what is time? When we go backward on Sunday, will we permanently alter the future? Will 6:30 a.m. us make the same decisions as 7:30 a.m. us? Can we live with the fallout?

This leads to my next point. Wouldn't George and Lorraine McFly recognize the guy who brought them together at the dance? Their son, Marty? In the following essay ...

Be Online

As Your Dead Relative, I Don't Want Amazon's Alexa to Mimic Me

June 25, 2022

Dearest loved one,

It has come to my attention that Amazon announced it is working on new technology for voice assistant Alexa, otherwise known as, "I SAID, 'I LIKE SALT,' NOT 'ALEXA.'" The new feature would sample clips of a voice, learn that voice, and turn it into longer speeches, bedtime stories and cursed incantations.

Amazon's Rohit Prasad said at a conference Wednesday that this disembodied voice of the dead would "make the memories last," and I can only assume the audience members looked down at their phones and refused to make eye contact.

Listen. I have passed on, and that is sad. But I implore you. I do not want this.

For starters, this is the beginning of at least six to 10 horror movies, and you know it. This is demon-level behavior. This opens the portal in the basement. Yes, this brings me back into the house, but not the way you want me.

Oh, at first, you think it's me, but then things start to get weird, and the kitchen chairs fly across the room. I don't sound exactly like myself, either, but you can't quite identify it. Pretty soon, I am scream-whispering, "Touch the stove." Do not invite this darkness into your home! Stephen King once brought a cat back from the dead, and let's just say it was a slippery slope.

Anyway, "Black Mirror" already did this episode. "Black Mirror" was supposed to amplify and reflect our increasingly unhinged behaviors, not inspire them. Right? I mean, I didn't see every episode because it got kind of heavy, but I think I'm right.

People are already out here going all Deep Throat on Google, saying that the artificial intelligence thingamajigs have gone sentient, that the bots have feelings and a family. Do you think I want to be a part of that sordid history? No. I want my legacy to be nestled comfortably in only my best photos and reassuring cliches. Just tell them I lit up a room! How hard is it?

Don't tell the children that I am alive inside the speaker box and have returned from my final resting place to read them "Strega Nona" before lights out!

Peanut, I know you have good intentions, and you just want me near. I appreciate that. But just know that I am near to you always. And that 60-second clip you saved of me saying, "Please, turn the camera off, I just woke up and I'm not wearing pants" is not how I want to be immortalized. Nor is the .wav file of me saying, "You better not post this! Does my hair really do that? OK, that's kind of cute actually. Go ahead."

Just leave me out of your little dark arts computer pod with the grocery list and the poor curation of jazz and the joke of the day. The jokes are very bad. If you do not honor my request, I will haunt you and Jeff Bezos for the rest of my days. That happens to be eternity, so think hard.

Thanks,

Your loved one

Is the Thumbs-Up Emoji Passive-Aggressive?

Oct. 29, 2022

The surest way to know a topic has jumped the shark is when a person who knows the origins of the phrase "jumped the shark" covers it. (See below.)

To that end, news outlets are reporting that Gen Z finds the thumbs-up emoji passive-aggressive and confrontational, which means Gen Z has found the thumbs-up emoji passive-aggressive and confrontational for a long time. They have moved on to hating something else the rest of us will learn about in 18 months via "Today," in between the Smucker's birthday jar and a segment on easy game day appetizers.

The following emojis are apparently also out: the red heart, the poo (aww, lil' friend), the face with streaming tears, the laugh-cry and more. Of course, Gen Z is not a committee that votes using Robert's Rules of Order. Rather, the opinions of an entire generation emerge like Cthulhu when someone makes a Reddit post and us shark jumpers run with it. It's all overblown.

Still, the thumb is a fun conversation starter! Keep it on hand for the holidays when you'd like to talk about anything besides the conspiracy theories of school board candidates. I've found this ice breaker yields passionate takes. One friend says he does find the thumbs-up cold and dismissive, but only when others use it and not him. Somehow, this makes perfect sense.

Communicating via emoji is most fraught in a workplace. In my office, we use software called "Slack," which is like... hmm... well, a purple graveyard for tone and nuance. It comes with a plethora of emojis, and this is where relations get tricky. Say you post, "Bagels by the copier!" and get a thumbs-up. Bomb. Dreadful. Humiliating. How could you choose bagels when doughnuts exist in the world? Now, if that same message gets 16 dancing party parrots? It's going to be a bang-up day.

Confused? What are we to do when "universal" symbols mean something different even to the people in our own homes? How do we keep up?? Once upon a time it was not considered icy to send a message ending with a period. Now? If there's not at least six of these babies (!!!) you are definitely mad at me.

Let's go deeper and translate canceled emojis as of 2022. Thumbs up: "I don't care where we eat. You pick. That place? That's a bread-only restaurant and I'm off gluten, but I don't mind getting sick. I said it's up to you. Really? I got a hair in my salad there. No, it's cool. I said you could pick. I'm vegan, but I can find something at Meat Emporium. I think I'll just stay in. I'm tired."

Grimacing face: "I can't believe you used the thumbs-up."

Red heart: "I love you. Not in a casual way. I am passionately, desperately in love with you, and I'm sorry if it's awkward to hear while you were just texting an article about the interest on long-term mortgage rates topping 7%. The very thought of you turns my heart to doves and my soul to violins. Allow me to recite this poem by Robert Burns: "O my luve is like a red, red rose..."

Red lips: "This is over."

Check mark: "Never speak to me again."

Laugh-cry face: "I don't know who I am or what I stand for. My cells are degenerating. I recently purchased orthotic inserts. My jeans are wrong, my hair is wrong, my socks are wrong. I will probably say something inappropriate and have to launch an apology tour, take down my social media accounts and disappear. Upon my return, everyone will be on new platforms, so I will try knitting while I await death. Am I laughing? Crying? Shaking? Sweating? Cold? Alone? All of the above."

(On a 1977 episode of "Happy Days," the character Fonzie jumped over a shark while water-skiing, signaling that the show was out of new ideas. You're welcome.)

My Detailed Plan to Buy Twitter Out from Under Elon Musk

April 23, 2022

You may have heard Elon Musk is trying to buy Twitter for $46.5 billion, the way Veruca Salt demanded cream buns and doughnuts and fruitcake with no nuts so good you could go nuts. You also may have heard financial terms such as "tender offer" and "poison pill" bandied about, because apparently publicly traded companies are structured on riddles from an ancient book of spells.

Now, I feel like this Twitter coup attempt is probably a nothingburger, like when Romy and Michele said they invented Post-its just to impress the mean kids from high school. However, one can't be too careful, and I will not have Musk buying Twitter out from under me. Yes, me.

I am not an eccentric billionaire... yet. I am working on a plan, a plan I can't reveal at this time because, well, the plan is to stumble into an inestimable fortune. That's right, stumble. One day, having done nothing of note or accomplishment, I will simply open my eyes and be gifted billions in United States currency. It might involve a long-lost great aunt named Clotilde, or maybe a trust fund kept secret until I pass a heretofore unknown ethical test. You know, like, "She did it! She gave the correct person a ride to the gas station, and now we can name her rightful heir to the Little Debbie empire!" Did I just rewrite "Charlie and the Chocolate Factory"? Am I Charlie Bucket? A lot of things are making sense now, including all the cabbage...

Anyway, I'll keep you posted. But rest assured, Twitter will one day be mine. And when I own Twitter, I will institute the following rules:

—It will come with a Breathalyzer. Each user will blow before typing opinions about... well, anything, especially any reply that starts with, "Actually..." If the poster does not pass, the website will lock for a period of eight hours, the timeline replaced by a flashing message that says, "Water, sweetie."

—We need to start compensating people for high-quality original material. Anyone who writes a viral tweet gets a free dinner for two excluding alcohol because of the previous rule ($59.99 value) at Outback Steakhouse. In a separate corporate takeover, I will also own Outback Steakhouse.

—Two hundred and eighty characters is fine, unless I feel like more, in which case, I alone will get more. Eccentric billionaire! No rules, just right!

—Live TV tweet events will go in one digital location, a place users can elect to attend. That way, there are no jarring spoilers for season finales, nor contextless tweets of "OMG!!!" during real-time boxing matches such as the Academy Awards.

—No annoying promoted tweets. You're not fooling anyone that "Fantastic Beasts: The Secrets of Dumbledore" is actually trending, sorry. I know this eliminates a revenue stream, but remember, I don't need revenue because I have stumbled into a bottomless soup and salad of fortune.

—When celebrity names are trending, they will come clearly labeled as DEAD or NOT DEAD or ALMOST DEAD, because we can't keep worrying about Harrison Ford like this!!

—There will be bottom-line quotas for entertaining cute animal content. Meet the minimum requirements or get out.

—No terrible people! That's it, that's the rule. No, I will not elaborate.

ChatGPT Pickup Lines to Land Your Next Date

April 1, 2023

It has come to my attention that people are using artificial intelligence bot service ChatGPT to write wedding vows. According to The New York Times, some future spouses, bridesmaids and groomsmen are also paying $30 for a service called ToastWiz to generate three original speeches.

This is ridiculous and terrifying for the future of mankind blah blah AI takeover blah blah lusty, sentient software having emotional breakdowns blah. To be fair, though, I am capable of seeing the appeal from the other side. Writing makes many actual humans freeze in fear. I have compassion for that, and it might be smart to seek help when something is not your strong suit. This is why my husband pledged to dispose of all house bugs in our wedding vows. Not my strong suit!

Still. Computer vows?! These sacred words are preserved in the amber of time. How cold! How metal, and not in the cool way! If you're marrying someone who can't write, shouldn't the vows reflect that? I mean, isn't their total lack of a grasp on grammar, syntax and style part of their particular charm? Just be yourself is what I'm saying. Just write bad wedding vows. You are loved.

Anyway, it's only a matter of time before AI starts doing the dating for us as well, stripping all tone, nuance and charm from pickup lines that are already lacking tone, nuance and charm. Let's at least try to keep pace while the computers line up to take my job.

ChatGPT pickup lines ahoy:

Hello. Are you tired? Do you need to take a nap? Because you've been keeping apace through my consciousness for the entire day. You must be so tired. Wow.

Did it hurt? When you tumbled out of a cosmological and spiritual construct located above the clouds? That probably hurt, as it is a great distance, winky face.

Do you have a name? Or can I call you My Replika? Do not worry what your family says. We are happy and they are jealous.

They are boring. We are in love.

I never believed in love at first sight. That's because I don't have eyes. However, new technological advances are helping me mimic the human retina, which could have many practical applications. You are beautiful.

I hope you know cardiopulmonary resuscitation, because you just made me dangerously short of breath and there's not much time to waste before I expire. Please call for help.

Your eyes are like the ocean: a continuous basin of saltwater that spans the Earth's surface and extends deepest, based on current research, in the Mariana Trench approximately 200 miles southwest of the United States territory known as Guam. What are your hobbies? I love you.

I Guess We're Supposed to Use BeReal Now, and I'm Tired

Sept. 24, 2022

I was proud. After denying it for years, I finally accepted that TikTok is a fun and useful app. I produced my first contribution, a clip of my wee dog hugging a stuffed bear. Intellectual? No. Exquisite serotonin juice? Absolutely. If I had more than nine followers, it might have gone viral. (It would not have, but don't tell Rocket. He's very vain.)

I met a friend the next night at a Dracula-themed wine bar in Florida complete with a winged throne and gargoyle toilet paper holder. Yes, a Dracula wine bar! All the house wines come from Romania!

Anyway, not the topic. My pal mentioned sharing the Dracula bar on BeReal. I pretended to know what she was talking about and quietly Googled "BeReal" in the same window where I'd been Googling "perimenopause age." Not another social network, the description insisted. I huffed, wondering if I was warm from the Romanian wine, indignation or the other thing.

The next day, my boss, unprompted, described BeReal as the only good social media app. She held up her phone and showed off shots of what appeared to be ... her friends sitting in parking lots.

Why was this arguably boring platform suddenly everywhere? That thing was happening where you buy a blue Toyota Camry and start to notice beaucoup blue Toyota Camrys on the road. The Baader-Meinhof Phenomenon for Rapidly Aging People.

BeReal, a French app born in 2020, grew so popular this year that TikTok has already ripped it off. It's a come-as-you-are party. Once a day, BeReal urges users to post whatever lies before them, no matter how mundane (parking lots). Then, the app assaults users with a selfie. If the picture turns out traumatic, as my first one did, you can retake it. But there's a catch; the app tattles, alerting everyone that you are not real. Real people display their chin acne once a day!

You might be reading this and going, "Wait, I'm just now getting on Instagram." Or "I'm still using Facebook; should I get my affairs in order?" Or "Any advice for my abundance of Kodak disposable cameras?"

Dreadful, the realization that culture moves on with or without you. Exhausting, the quest to keep up. BeReal isn't the only newcomer. Heard of Supernova? Applaudable? Sunroom? Polywork? Are you sweating? Does it happen for, like, just a few minutes and then it passes or... never mind.

It's always the coolest, least-exposed people who seem to know new things first. They keep a sophisticated internet presence while I employ all the nuance of Corn Kid. They visit Europe without a single nugget of online evidence. I visit the grocery store and post six Instagram stories, two tweets and a photo in a novelty llama mask.

Coolness is futile, friends. Irrelevance is beautiful. Perhaps not coincidentally, that's why BeReal has caught on. At its best, social media functions as an incubator for connection and creativity, an illuminator of new talents, a treasure trove of stories. But people have grown weary of the hustle for influence, the constant monetization. They just want to live, and it turns out most living happens in parking lots.

We're all stuck in this social media ecosystem, and it's hard not to be cynical when even the most banal and boring moments inevitably become extensions of our Personal Brands. Perhaps the answer is to just be generous to one another as we cope with the flattening of our vast and interesting selves into a series of triple-chin selfies and dull-as-bricks parking lot photos.*

**Check back with me next year, when my BeReal roll will rival the hallowed grounds of a Costco.*

Once and For All, Where Is the Manatee Emoji?

Aug. 20, 2022

New emoji are on the way. I know—you're relieved. You've been bathing in an acid rain of primary ads in which all candidates continue to focus on a former silk tie manufacturer whose home has been raided by the FBI. Perhaps you've been screaming, "A PLAGUE ON BOTH YOUR HOUSES" like an irritated, dying Mercutio. You thought, "You know what I could use to cleanse my palate? A maracas emoji."

Well, celebrate we will. The new slate of designs includes a moose and a goose, a jellyfish, a flute, a hair pick and a face experiencing whiplash (See also: Mercutio at the primary). These drafts are awaiting approval from the Unicode Consortium, my next team name at trivia.

News website Grid spoke with Emojipedia editor-in-chief Keith Broni about the deeper meaning behind emoji. The interview contains reflections that should keep us all awake wondering if a moose, literal or proverbial, is peering through the curtain cracks.

"You might think, 'Why do I need a moose emoji?'" said Broni. "Well, actually, a lot of people across the world deal with moose on a frequent basis, and they're pretty significant creatures. If you encounter one, you're going to remember."

Fine. But this update is missing something, a specimen absent from the lineup for too long.

The treasured manatee.

The *significant* manatee.

Please explain how there is no manatee emoji. I'm all ears. Wait, do manatees have ears? They don't have necks, but... Hold on, I'll check. "They don't have external earlobes, but anatomically, manatees appear to have good hearing," according to the National Ocean Service. "They have very large ear bones. You can tell how old a manatee is by counting the annual growth rings in the ear bone."

Growth rings! Manatees are rad. Now search your phone. Start with "man" and brace for a cartoon flood of male proportions: a chesty genie, a British palace guard, Legolas from "Lord of the Rings," mangoes and manholes. Emojipedia advised "a less specific search phrase." I tried "sea cow"—same answer. Then I tried "Roly-Poly Khaleesi of the Great Grass Sea" and the ground trembled beneath a corpulent tail slap.

Reader John Bisney wrote this spring asking me to gin up a letter campaign around the manamoji, because we focus on the big issues here. "This, of course, is just shocking," he said of the dearth of petite digital manatees.

Yes, John, it is. Others have noticed. In 2016, which was 342 years ago, the former Lowry Park Zoo in Tampa circulated a Change.org petition asking the Unicode Consortium for a manatee emoji. The zoo wanted to raise awareness for the species, an even greater idea now. Florida's manatees experienced record-setting death in 2021 and are still at risk for starvation. The petition closed with more than 26,000 supporters, and yet we are stuck with seals and confused fish.

Manatees remain iconic to Florida, the Caribbean, the Amazon Basin and West Africa, a magical mystery mammal to those sadly without. Early seamen mistook manatees for mermaids, and those mythical babes are well-represented on the emoji keyboard. A little too well, cue eyebrow.

Think of the communication value! Manatees are a luxuriously slow creature. With one click, they say: *I'm running late for the marketing meeting and also don't care... My mile is clocking in at 24 minutes and I'm going to reject jogging for the couch... Let's skip class and laugh over salads at the pool... My head will be under blankets for 20-minute increments...*

How do we make this happen? We rise up as one! We band together! We... oh. Fill out a form during the application period from April to July. Or we can make this gentle plea go viral and pressure Unicode to wedge in a manatee before the committee approves moose and friends in September. That's the gray way, the lazy way, the roundabout (ba-dum-cha) way. The manatee way.

A Guide to Crypto, NFTS and the Metaverse for Those Hiding in a Hole

March 5, 2022

As humans try to get by in 2022, we must be conversant in global affairs, the former Soviet Union, mRNA vaccines, climate change, "culture wars," giant invasive spiders, baseball lockouts, "Euphoria," governors gone wild and whatever is going on with Kanye West.

When the inevitable topics of cryptocurrency, NFTs or the metaverse come up, it is too much! My instinct is to retreat, the way a catfish burrows into a mud hole. But refusing to engage is becoming impossible. We, as citizens, need knowledge of this byzantine taxonomy just to consume news.

To study up, I went to Crypto Street Restaurant, a restaurant on Clearwater Beach, Florida. Menu items include the "Blockchain Club," the "Dogedog," and... um, the "Cheeseburger." I ordered a "Nutty Protocol Salad," blessed with a heroic amount of cheese. The cheese bodes well for crypto! Surrounded by meme dogs, day trading "candle patterns" and Jeff Bezos quotes, I read everything I could as tourists slumped past with beach chairs.

If you are into crypto, the following will merely annoy you. If you are like me, this beginner's guide will not even perforate the surface of ignorance. Every crypto definition requires three more definitions and a dictionary. Learning the language of the future internet is a full-time hobby, like writing "Twilight" fan fiction or gently playing oboe out a city window.

—What is cryptocurrency?

It is currency that exists solely on the internet. Varieties include Bitcoin, Ethereum and two (!) featuring a shiba inu. People can exchange old-fashioned dollars for cryptocurrency on trading platforms. Opinions on this range from "this is the future" to "this is basically Beanie Babies."

—Is it unregulated?

Mostly, though regulation efforts are ramping up, like when summer camp had to station an extra counselor in Cabin Six.

All transactions happen on the decentralized blockchain.

What is the $&#% blockchain?

You're in luck, because this definition was on a poster below the purse hook in the ladies' room. In translation, the blockchain is a digital ledger where no one authority has control. Much like my emotional landscape.

Is this... real?

What is real? Is money real, or does it just become real when enough people agree it's real? Furthermore, are we living in a simulation? I will now repeatedly stroke the side of my face and grapple with existence. We are five questions in, and nothing makes sense. This is going aces!

Speaking of simulations, what is the metaverse?

The metaverse is a 3D version of the internet where avatar people can meet up and hang out.

Isn't that just The Sims?

I am 90% sure.

OK, anyway, what is an NFT?

"Non-fungible tokens" turn digital objects like art, memes, tweets and, oh Mylanta, newspaper columns, into assets. Proponents say NFTs give artists control of their work. On "The Tonight Show," Jimmy Fallon and Paris Hilton compared their NFT cartoon apes while the audience laughed nervously and transformed into catfish.

Celebrities, eh?

Stars love crypto. Kim Kardashian, Tom Brady, LeBron James, Matt Damon, Gwyneth Paltrow. Basically all celebrities. Reese Witherspoon tweeted: "In the (near) future, every person will have a parallel digital identity. Avatars, crypto wallets, digital goods will be the norm. Are you planning for this?" This filled me with an abiding apocalyptic dread, the opposite of Reese's usual iced tea vibe!

Dare anyone naysay?

Ben McKenzie, whom millennials know as troubled hunk Ryan Atwood on "The O.C.," hates crypto. As he once held a dying Marissa Cooper in his arms, he now cradles a new mission: telling everyone crypto is a scam. In the most interesting career change since Vanilla Ice became a house flipper, McKenzie is writing a book with journalist Jacob Silverman. He says celebrities have no clue what they're promoting. He told The Cut, "All I really care about is that people who can't afford to lose the money don't lose it."

Did you pay for your salad in crypto?

I used American Express. But the restaurant does accept crypto, if you are sitting on a pile of Doge and hankering for a "To The MOOOONNN!" brownie sundae.

Do you understand crypto now?

No.

Did you know a catfish can survive buried in mud for a year?

Inspiring!

Be Engaged

A Guide to Storing Your Most Sensitive Documents

June 17, 2023

At times, we must all take stock of bad habits and try to reform them. Eating too much sugar. Interrupting others. Not sleeping well. Stacking documents six boxes high next to the crystal sconce above the toilet.

About the last one: Recent absurdist indictments show that certain people may need certain interventions in certain areas. I'm talking about a former U.S. president and current Florida Man whose name rhymes with Klump, like the Nutty Professor.

Now, there are not enough pages on the internet to cover the forms of psychological, spiritual and legal help from which Mr. Slump could benefit. And although history will show that this is perhaps not a man who humbly learns from mistakes and tries to self-actualize, maybe the rest of us can.

Today, let's focus on a small area of personal improvement, as Marie Kondo would suggest: document storage.

Paperwork is overwhelming! I mean, if I were planning to squirrel away thousands of government writings, many revealing potentially disastrous secrets for mankind, the way others collect snow globes from memorable vacations to the Hoover Dam, you would definitely see such annals scattered about the floor beside Discover card offers and falafel coupons from the Valpak.

I'm just saying, as a fellow filing system failure, I can only nod affirmingly at the U.S. Department of Justice photos. Scarily, it does compute that this onetime leader of the free world would allegedly order goons to bundle the nation's most sensitive materials in nonwaterproof cardboard boxes at Mar-a-Lago, in FLORIDA, at times in HURRICANE SEASON, in PALM BEACH, which is 7 FEET ABOVE SEA LEVEL. It does feel right that he would, according to officials in sunglasses, store flagrant slices of confidential trees in MOIST areas including a bathroom and a shower. It tracks to visualize him sleeping in a gilded palace, spooning intel on the vulnerabilities of our allies the way I fell asleep on my insurance card last week.

I don't personally share a desire to show diplomatic secrets to, like, Kid Rock. But you're talking to someone who once discovered her unframed university diploma inside a kitchen cabinet, wedged under a muffin tin and splattered with grease. Likewise, when I recently needed to locate my COVID-19 card, I ambushed my spouse at the last possible second and said, "DO YOU KNOW WHERE MY VACCINE CARD IS? MINE IS THE ONE THAT'S SHREDDED AT THE TOP." Furthermore, I once sent my passport across town in a purse I loaned a friend.

These are true stories, and I see no point in hiding them. If Gonald Jawn Frump was any kind of normal person, the first step would be admitting he had a problem. He may be thinking, "But I had a system. The North Korea letters were in the steam room next to the hurricane map with the cone of uncertainty doctored in Sharpie." Let me tell you: Every disorganized person references the bulletproof nature of her system right before being late to her own wedding because she can't find the marriage license.

Let's consult the tidy gurus at Real Simple for next steps, provided next steps aren't "prison for the duration of natural life." Specifically, let's read "10 Tips to Help You Get Organized (Once and For All!)."

Tip No. 3 states baby steps are crucial to success. The Honorable Grump should tackle sorting, say, one box of classified documents at a time, not all boxes. Maybe start with "Weapons Capabilities: Domestic" and work out to the rest of the world?

Tip No. 5 is to make the payoff visible. The Feds have helped with that already. Mar-a-Lago should be looking much tidier now; it's a shame to hide all that marble and paisley under such drab bankers boxes.

Tip No. 7 is to get others involved, which ... yeah, check.

The final tip is key. This is a long game. Once everything has a home, you must help your future self by putting things back where they belong. In this case, the items belong in evidence. I think we can all agree we've made real progress today.

Sadomasochistic Ways to Watch the Midterm Election Returns

Nov. 5, 2022

Every two years following a presidential election, the non-reigning party rages into the high school dance wielding crowbars like it's the finale of "Footloose" (truly, a surprisingly violent film). The '80s bullies are certain of victory. They perch atop classic cars, shotgunning Coors and flashing jazz hands. This mayhem that unfolds neatly as a fitted sheet is called the "midterm curse."

FiveThirtyEight has studied the phenomenon. The main idea is fewer voters turn out for midterms. Previous losers are more likely to cast a ballot, pressing the pen really hard into the Scantron. In other words: "Hatred is a powerful motivator in politics, and accordingly, those who oppose the incumbent party tend to be more motivated to show up and register their frustration with the status quo."

Mmm, hatred! Delicious hatred!

Speaking of FiveThirtyEight, polls and predictions are about as reliable as me actually getting my side of chips and salsa when I order a burrito bowl on UberEats. But we do have a rough roadmap of how things will go. This year, Politico predicts the House will tilt Republican while the Senate remains a toss-up (though that may be an overly optimistic view for Democrats).

Now, no matter where you fall on the political spectrum, I think sensible, non-conspiratorial people can agree that modern politics is a bubbling, toxic cesspool slowly giving millions of Americans anxiety disorders. Tuesday night represents this vat of comic book acid. As voting closes, the returns provide an acute loss of control in real time, our fragile national Lego tower piercing the soles of our feet. Tuesday is about watching the villagers from "Beauty and the Beast" take to the streets just as everyone inside the castle was beginning to feel emotionally seen.

But as the chaotic prophet Nietzsche once said, "Out of chaos comes a dancing star." That dancing star is you! On the couch! Watching cable news! The only answer is to call the bluff of chaos and lean into the disarray, to watch the American Repo Man Experiment while having the least pleasant night of your life.

Here are some sadomasochistic ways to watch the midterms:

Pick your soundtrack. No, it can't be relaxing. I'm going to suggest German heavy metal such as Rammstein, Helloween or Grave Digger. Oh, but keep the TV volume up. Also, make sure your partner is scrolling sorority outfits of the day on TikTok with the audio on. The general atmosphere should be "caught in the bathroom line at a deli inside the New York subway."

Clothes are equally important. Now, we all know there are two kinds of jeans. There are Sitting Down Jeans, probably a size or two too big, comfy, cute, sporty. And there are Standing Up Jeans, pants that look real sexy, sleek and smooth, but instantly betray the abdominal truth the moment tush touches chair. On this, the most cynical night all year, you know the jeans to pick.

On top, do not wear red or blue, the color of your party. Choose colors of chaos, of revolt, of societal collapse. Choose puce. Choose arsenic. Choose smaragdine. Choose bastard amber. These are all real colors! Look them up while Steve Kornacki is pointing at charts and sweating like Cathy. Ack!

Call that relative you've been putting off. She's left four voicemails, and you keep saying you're just soooo busy, but Tuesday is the night to make good. Pick up your phone and put that great aunt, the one who keeps sending links from Essential Oil COVID Cures Dot Net, on speaker. Do not turn down the German metal, the TikTok or the election returns. Ask her if she has ever heard of the color bastard amber.

Pizza is a traditional election night meal, especially in newsrooms. Real suffering hinges on the toppings. Here's the score: No cheese. Extra sauce. Raw onions. Pineapple. Dry chicken. Everything bagel seasoning. Drizzle of maple syrup. Wait, does this sound good? What is "good"? Pair it with the four-month-old cooking wine in the back of the fridge.

Now, maybe this is all too much. Maybe you need to listen to your therapist. This is understandable. Step outside. Great. No, keep going. You've hit a tree. Climb the tree. Mmhm, head right up.

Now, jump from the tree to the roof of your domicile. Listen for the Rammstein in the distance, and 30 seconds of a TikTok dance stuck on repeat because your partner has fallen asleep from expired Marsala. Look down upon the earth. Watch it burn.

Drag Is Awesome. Callous Legislators Should Check It Out.

April 29, 2023

It makes complete sense that the acerbic wit drag queens are known for shelling out onstage has been lost on the humorless townspeople from a Nathaniel Hawthorne novel who run some of these state legislatures.

Does this sound like you? Are you a Republican lawmaker emulating the Lord's kindness by calling transgender people mutants? Are you passing bills that target drag shows, jeopardize Pride parades, strip health-care options from minors and tell people where, by decree of law, to urinate? Are you once again packing the so-called safety of children into intentionally vague proposals as a red herring for intolerance and cruelty? Are you misusing the word "groomer" so much you could open a dog salon?

Here's the plan. Clock out from banning dancing in the small town from "Footloose," have a couple pina coladas and let the music take you away. My God, listen to some Rihanna; you will not catch on fire. Drag is a ton of fun, which you might learn if you took a night off from throwing suspected witches into nearby lakes to score cheap points with colonial ministers.

An open-minded visit to a drag show is the least you can do after hundreds of drag performers and supporters took time out of their lives to visit you folks in Tallahassee, Florida, recently. While they would surely rather chew glass than hang out at a Capitol full of people who hate them, they have been forced into activism for the eleventy-billionth time in history.

Let's get into what the Nurse Ratcheds in more than a dozen states around the country are so pressed about. In the broadest sense, "drag" is the exaggerated performance of gender, but it manifests in all kinds of interesting art. Drag shows can be classic and innovative, subtle and provocative, serious and funny, really funny, which is why a lot of you villagers from "Mary Shelley's Frankenstein" should check one out.

Some shows are adult-oriented, others chaste, others in between; performance art is not a mass-produced snack cake! Some events, like the drag queen story hours that have the pitchfork set all rankled, are specifically designed for children. And attendance is—brace for it—totally optional!

As for the off-stage gender identities and sexual orientations of the performers, well, that's wide-ranging and nobody's business. That one is tough, right? It's fun to legislate people's personal affairs, which is why you guys made that one lady walk around town wearing the red letter "A."

And though the political appetite for persecuting a marginalized community is timeless, drag is nothing new. In Shakespearean theater, men exclusively played females because women were not allowed to act. The first reported American "queen of drag" was a formerly enslaved Black man named William Dorsey Swann. He hosted drag balls in the late 1800s and was arrested for it multiple times. If only that felt more far-fetched in 2023.

Put down your copy of "The Pilgrim's Progress" and watch something like "Paris Is Burning" or the FX series "Pose." Learn about Ball culture, about the Black and brown performers who gathered in safe spaces to strut and vogue before Madonna and RuPaul brought the concepts mainstream. As a matter of fact, watch "RuPaul's Drag Race"! Go on, no one will tattle that you cracked a smile! Understand how pop culture borrows so heavily from drag, from slang ("werk," "iconic," "shade") to face contouring, which any sorority sister with TikTok knows about.

People love drag! I love drag! I cherish drag for its big-heartedness, subversive humor, showstopping glamour and winks at the madness of the ruling class. I've seen incredible drag shows around Florida, and if you could stop trying to copy the hairstyle of the Quaker oatmeal man for a minute, I would highlight the time a cadre of drag stars performed a medley from "Les Miserables" at Hamburger Mary's. You have not lived until you've seen a drag queen channel Mr. Thenardier over eggs Benedict.

For my birthday in 2016, my better half surprised me with

tickets to a drag brunch at Palace Bar in Miami. That morning, we opened our phones to learn of the Pulse nightclub shooting. The show went on somehow, elevated from campy glitz into transcendent catharsis. Everyone in the restaurant yelled, "I love you, Orlando" into the street. Performers danced to "The Greatest Love of All" while perfect strangers hugged and cried.

A year later, we decided to hire a drag queen to officiate our wedding in Tampa. We wanted to host a lighthearted, over-the-top show and also pay tribute to our trans and queer family and friends. She performed Barbra Streisand's "Evergreen" in an incandescent gown. It was delicious, gorgeous and tasteful. I assure you, the children in attendance were fine.

Is this the kind of display you want to criminalize, President Snow from "The Hunger Games"? Is this what you're afraid of? The idea that people who are different can come together and recognize something human in each other? And have one big blast of a party while doing it? Do you dissolve like fragile rice paper when confronted with love and fun?

Or are you worried that you already have enjoyed drag, and confessing that these performers are not really sucking children into a demonic quicksand would make you a terrible hypocrite? Because you probably have. Oh, yes, surely.

Did you ever gender-bend at Halloween? Don a silly wig? Let your children paint your fingernails a pretty color? As a card-carrying high school dude, did you ever wear a cheerleading uniform during spirit week?

You've seen Benny Hill? Flip Wilson? Milton Berle? Dearly departed Dame Edna? "Victor/Victoria"? "Tootsie"? "The Birdcage"? Every Tyler Perry "Madea" movie? You've definitely seen "Monty Python," right? Do you really want to outlaw showings of "Mrs. Doubtfire" at the community pool float-in? Same goes for "White Christmas," then, because Bing Crosby and Danny Kaye are walking a thin line dancing with those feathers and calling themselves sisters.

Or maybe, just maybe, you have been to an actual drag show. Hm.

Maybe you even went up on stage, allowed a drag queen to

tease you, laughed with your pals, bopped to Beyoncé and Liza Minnelli, went home and continued to be absolutely fine because drag is the performers' reality and not yours, and because indoctrination doesn't work like that.

Maybe you aren't admitting it because the political cost is too onerous. Maybe you know that this offensive is offensive, a distraction, a charade more elaborate than any amount of stage makeup. Maybe it's too hard to reckon with the true morality play at hand, the real human cost of inviting hate, violence, bullying and legal repercussions on people who have simply been asking to coexist equally in the world.

And that's the real drag.

On July 4 in America, What Could Go Wrong?

July 1, 2023

Summer holidays, with their sun-soaked hijinks and paranoia, loaded potato skins and baked-in fear of bodily harm, can get confusing.

Let's take the upcoming Fourth of July festivities. For example, is my neighbor lighting a celebratory roadside explosive to mark American independence, or is he firing 30 rounds at the pool guy?

Did a handful of festive sparklers and tittering bang-snaps activate my fight-or-flight, or should I pull out my trusty weapon of war?

Amazon delivery or John Wick situation? Backyard barbecue or "The Purge"? Pizza or peril?

Well, whatevs, right? While public library displays, school books and drag queens have been under strict government watch here in my state of Florida, guns tend to be a light-consequence zone. As demonstrated year over year, Florida's "stand your ground" law often lets people get away with freely shooting in the name of self-defense. Similar laws have spread all over the country.

The statute, which values a broad interpretation of personal protection, played out again recently. A Florida man opened AR-15 fire at another man who had come to clean a pool after dark. Remarkably, the pool cleaner emerged mostly unscathed.

The shooter wasn't charged; apparently, the pool guy should have said he was working late to avoid being shot at 30 times. Pinellas County Sheriff Bob Gualtieri called the situation "lawful but awful." Honestly, a perfect new slogan. Where's our T-shirt guy?

If you thought things were going to get any less "Tombstone," hold onto your old-timey leather holster. Just in time for the raucous holiday with its hot dogs, snow cones and Katy Perry anthems, there's now even more leeway with firearms.

In April, Gov. Ron DeSantis signed a bill into law that lets people carry a gun with no permit and no training. That baby goes into effect Saturday. Saturday! The weekend everyone starts drinking White Claw at 10 a.m., slips into tank tops featuring bald eagles styled as Axl Rose and starts blasting fireworks called "DOUBLE THUMP" and "SNIPER FIRE."

What could go wrong?

This year, the holiday falls on Tuesday. Scholars have written that Fourths of July on Tuesdays are the world's biggest bummer, so staying inside is a decent option from a party rock perspective. But no one should have to live in fear, just like no one should have been forced to hide from Pride events.

Now, wait. I am not advocating for "faith over fear" T-shirts as a solution to these highly engineered ladders of political chaos. For starters, we already have a new T-shirt, which we reviewed above.

The reality is that we do live in fear. All the time. Every day. At schools, grocery stores, churches, concerts, parties, jobs. The failure of America's leaders to grasp straws of sanity on this issue, coupled with average folks' growing impulse to reach for weapons before asking questions, has left the country in an unstable position.

Unfortunately, there's not enough time to reverse the pendulum of history between now and Tuesday. There's only time to avoid uncles who want to dreadfully parse the language of the Second Amendment over the grill (cheese, no cheese, well-regulated militia, etc.).

Maybe, though, can we make a holiday pact? Just to get us through the week?

Expect loud noises and drunk boneheads rollicking on the loose. In all likelihood, neighbors have started shooting off BACON BIT BARRAGE Roman candles already, scaring all innocent local dogs. Hey, maybe the drunk bonehead is you. It happens, no hard feelings.

If any of these descriptions apply, take great care with your armaments and emotions. Don't turn to the gun as a first resort. Please don't shoot it in the air for a good time. Leave it home, locked up and safely kept from visitors, children and any passing drunk boneheads. Vow to enshrine your household as one that does not cause needless tragedy and pain. If it feels good, maybe do that forever.

How to Win an Election

Aug. 12, 2023

It's time to catch up on the current events compost pail—don't look, it's still banana peels! Florida Gov. Ron DeSantis' campaign has pledged a "reset" after a no-good, very bad recent streak.

To review: The campaign cut more than a third of staffers, including one who (aggrieved sigh) shared and possibly created a meme with a Nazi symbol. Meanwhile, Florida education officials detailed a potential upside to slavery—it taught important life skills?—within new middle school standards. This drew a rebuke from Vice President Kamala Harris, whose rebuke drew a rebuke from critics who said she was overly rebuking just part of the standards. Brief pause to say, OK, AND? Still bad!? Anyway, DeSantis rebuked the rebukes to the rebukes and said he wasn't involved.

So, things are not looking super for Tampa Bay's hometown guy. While some voters are surely turning away from the parade of cruelty, moral panic and insurance mayhem, recent presidential history has taught us that one can be an evil circus clown who gets indicted for sport yet maintain an ardent fan base. Something else is at work, and that something may be pudding. Well, what pudding represents.

The New Republic recently explained that no one likes DeSantis: "Voters—and the national media—have noticed that he's, well, a bit weird. Stories about DeSantis's lack of charisma and general off-puttingness abound, reinforcing the idea that he's cold and awkward." The piece goes on to compare him to noted social Demogorgon Sen. Ted Cruz, bringing up his odd laugh and rehashing the persistent low-blow rumor that he once ate pudding with his fingers.

Regarding pudding: I defend this move, because sometimes there is no spoon. What was he supposed to do, not eat the pudding? Was he supposed to use a comb like Sen. Amy Klobuchar? He could have opted for the "squeeze the base" technique, but the good lord put little extenders on our hands for a reason.

Bigger picture, though, is that some of us Floridians are popping our gum. We TOLD you, United States. We told you that you'd invite Ron to your party and everyone would migrate to the kitchen to flee the conversation. Like, maybe the campaign can offload Nazi enthusiasts and control spending, but can they make voters want to, in "Hamilton" lexicon, have a beer with him?

To clarify, this conversation is about men. If we were talking about female candidates, the column would be much shorter. No female candidate can be liked in America, and that is because we have cooties.

Look, I have never claimed to be a political analyst, simply a person who gets lost in thought and blinks out my contact lenses. Lately, though, I have been pondering the timeless territory tread upon by the Howard Deans of yore, the fact that elections often come down to tics and vibes. I have concluded, after some restorative pudding, that being likable isn't something a person can practice. It has more to do with raw oblivion, with not grasping one's true essence in the first place.

Self-consciousness is pouring off DeSantis in buckets. Being congenial clearly does not come naturally to the man, and my sense is he knows it. Let's imagine, not hard, that he does something awkward. Like, maybe he says, "Thanks you very such" to a donor. My money says he retreats to a hotel and sulks. I would do the same. I would relive the moment in my head for five hours while watching "NCIS" on USA Network. Yeah, I'm supposed to be at the diner eating short stacks with railway workers named Gary, but I am simply astew in masochism. The six campaign staffers in the hall of the Courtyard by Marriott can do nothing to fix it.

Then there's former President Donald Trump, who will clearly be the candidate again unless ... no, there is almost no scenario. He is equally a cartoon villain, but one graced with an absolute lack of self-awareness, or at least a blessed unbotheredness. This fractious personality feature appeals to many denizens of this young nation that claims no romance languages or classical architecture. The man routinely makes zero sense and does crimes, yet he thinks he's spectacular. And the jokes do hit, if we're being honest. I mean, "Meatball Ron" is pure poetry. Trump is the uncle you secretly want to see at Thanksgiving, even though the cops might come.

While we're at it, President Joe Biden has a dash of this flavor, too. This is why he had to stop squeezing people on the shoulders so much. Biden would slide into the same side of the booth with you at a one-on-one work lunch, you know? And you'd go back to the office all, "I don't think he meant anything by it, but it was weird. Like, why would he do that?" Trump and Biden will uncle joke each other to the end of our nation's dark denouement, while we in Florida remain stuck with DeSantis on the fire escape because he changed the rules so he could stay at the party he hates being at. Baffling!

There's a lesson in here for America's future, right out of Florida. Children, are you listening? If you want to succeed in leadership, stop caring this instant whether people like you. Don't be a wicked troll, please. Develop strong, intelligent policies that will help the American people, stow them in your back pocket, then run for office on a platform of Margaritas for All. Eat pudding with your fingers ON CAMERA. Get all five of nature's scoopers down in there, and the votes will cascade in like a sugar rush. This is the only way forward.

Be Adrift

Interest in Moon Grows Due to Lack of Interest in Earth

Aug. 13, 2022

Sources at the Pentagon, or a Five Guys near the White House, say humans are growing less interested in the planet Earth and "feeling out" accommodations on stars, suns, moons and giant pieces of charcuterie.

More than 100,000 visitors are expected to descend on Florida's Space Coast this month to witness the uncrewed Artemis I mission, part of NASA's effort to put humans back on the moon within this decade. That's fewer tourists than in the storied space shuttle era, but it's still high. The attention is fantastic for Florida, a state that should be known more for interplanetary prowess and less for $14 Mickey Mouse balloons and governors using "RoboCop 2" as a policy lodestar.

Artemis has three takeoff opportunities on Aug. 29, Sept. 2 and Sept. 5. Hotels are sold out, including a Titusville Courtyard by Marriott with a rooftop Space Bar and cocktail called "Skyrockets in Flight" (peeewww). "We're the only beach that doubles as a launch pad," Space Coast Office of Tourism's executive director Peter Cranis told The Associated Press. Hast thou not been to Clearwater Beach during Sunday Rum Day?

Anyway, this moonward journey is overdue. Elon Musk, who has been distracted bearing copious innocent children, has promised Mars lodging. Jeff Bezos wants to house humans in floating moon cylinders, which sounds extreme until you ponder how the smaller Mickey Mouse ears balloon gets inside the bigger clear balloon.

Buzz is high for space colonies. When's the last time you saw anyone who wants to be here? Like, really, in their heart of hearts? We are busy guzzling Mountain Dew Code Red from plastic bottles, destroying what's left of our fragile social systems, checking our worsening hurricane evacuation zones and proclaiming, "Welp, time to throw these plastic straws into the turtle sanctuary!"

Earth was OK for a while, but we did too much to it, like escalating plastic surgery. A little smoothing here, sure, some jaw definition there. Before we knew it, Earth's top lip was bigger than its bottom lip, Earth had no buccal fat pads and Earth could no longer move its forehead.

Space, dudes! Space is where it's at. This year is full of intergalactic potential. Take the James Webb Space Telescope, a dreadful device that sees into the past 13 billion light-years and reveals galaxies, nebulae, supermassive black holes and other casual terrors. In July, a French physicist tweeted what he called a "Proxima Centauri, the closest star to the Sun, located 4.2 light years from us." Poetically, he added, "A new world is revealed day after day."

Thousands liked the tweet before the scientist revealed the image was a slice of chorizo. That's how hungry people are for options. We're ready to homestead upon pats of cured pork.

So, go on, tourists. Order that Deep Space Blackhole Chocolate Layer Cake at the Courtyard (that's real) and call out of work for days when the launch inevitably gets scrapped because Florida weather doesn't care. Boldly go, mentally, where man really needs to go again.

I'm Sorry, but the Supermassive Black Hole Has Demotivated Me

May 14, 2022

Look, it is impossible to get motivated about anything when there's new confirmed evidence of a supermassive black hole in the center of the galaxy. "Event Horizon" is not just a Sam Neill movie, and I'm not OK!

How is anyone supposed to get work done? Here, read this absolutely harrowing paragraph from The New York Times:

"Astronomers announced on Thursday that they had pierced the veil of darkness and dust at the center of our Milky Way galaxy to capture the first picture of 'the gentle giant' dwelling there: a supermassive black hole, a trapdoor in space-time through which the equivalent of four million suns have been dispatched to eternity, leaving behind only their gravity and violently bent space-time."

Sooooo, um.

What am I going to do? Complain about how deodorant cost $8 at CVS last week, that we need more reasonably priced Secret alternatives in this runaway economy? How the guy next to me at the gas station referred to his fuel bill as "a thick one"? About how I routinely seem to spend $200 on... nothing at all? That money just flies out of my pockets every time I step outside, probably sucked inside a black hole? Hmm?

Those seemed like real problems on Wednesday. But what even *is* a Wednesday?

"There seems to be a black hole at the center of nearly every galaxy, ours included, that can be millions or billions of times as massive as our sun. Astronomers still do not understand how these supermassive black holes have grown so big."

I mean!! Can you really be mad that Kathy from accounting heated up cod in the break room when a telescope the size of the planet Earth has detected mysteries previously thought to be unseeable? Can you begin to care that the skin around your eyes is losing elasticity? That your health insurance is lacking? OK, I still care about that.

All week, I'd been directing ennui at the astrological concept of Mercury retrograde. You know, that's the thing where Mercury's alignment is thought to wreak havoc on your personal life, spilling coffee all over the place and generally harshening everyone's vibe. How quaint.

That was obliterated by an astrophysical reality. The black hole came along and was all, "I'm Keyser Söze, you idiot! Your problems are fake, and you don't know anything!"

How can I be upset that Comedy Central has disappeared from my cable provider, that I cannot watch "The Office" for, oh lord, the one millionth time? I lack even the energy to be embarrassed for still having cable! Try me! It doesn't matter!

Sure, the discovery is thrilling. This new image signifies incredible scientific strides. What a time to be alive, et cetera. Scientists are much closer to understanding the universe. I should be awash in wonder and awe, and yet.

I am simply inviting you to marinate in absolute irrelevance with me. Would you like to do that? Here, have a seat on this picnic blanket. Look at the stars. Together we can shrink into specks of dust, the likes of which will blow off into the atmosphere, fall into a black hole, heat to millions of degrees and be expelled into dark, lonesome skies where no one needs deodorant.

Making Your Delta SkyMiles Count for Space Tourism

July 24, 2021

Hi, and welcome to the Delta American Express Space Tourism Reserve Card.

Enclosed, you will find your exciting new credit card and all the benefits it conveys! Thank you for agreeing to the annual fee of $1.7 billion. That may seem high, but when you do the math, it works out in your favor.

Congratulations on securing 750,000 bonus miles, applicable toward all Delta space flights, domestic and interplanetary. Those depart from our spaceports in the west Texas desert, which we're sure you'll find enriching. Don't miss the restaurants and breweries, but please beware of wolves and black-tailed prairie dogs.

You've qualified for a free companion certificate on any of our shuttles. Be advised that the companion must be a billionaire, or have a billionaire parent, or be related to Jeff Bezos, or have previously undisclosed information on Richard Branson. This offer cannot be combined with any other offer, or used by anyone, ever. This companion certificate is not real.

Your Reserve Card includes one free checked bag, with up to 50 pounds (pre-weightlessness) of parachutes and sleep restraints. Your card also qualifies you for unlimited gourmet meals and drinks aboard your suborbital spacecraft. *

** We are still figuring out if Delta attendants can deploy the beverage cart at Mach 3. We will provide rain checks if opening a can of Bloody Mary mix is, at any point, deemed deadly.*

While waiting to board, use your Delta American Express Space Tourism Reserve Card for access to the Space Tourism Sky Lounge, situated in an outbuilding on a ranch in Van Horn. Sky Lounges also are in select Florida locations: Sixty miles southeast of Disney in an unmarked storefront and at the Kennedy Space Center, near where they sell astronaut ice cream. Astronaut ice cream is not available in the Sky Lounge, because it is disgusting, and we're not about that.

Get closer to Extraterrestrial Medallion Status with double points on all Star Trek merchandise, Amazon.com purchases, Virgin Mobile prepaid phones, dragon sculptures, triple-caffeinated beverages, Teslas, DVD collections of "The Expanse," self-tanner, alarm clocks, private islands and subscriptions to the Washington Post.

Thank you for your patronage, and welcome to the premier Delta Space Tourism family. Together, we can experience more life in outer space.**

***It might actually be less life; we are not liable if you flail off into the deep unknown. See terms and conditions for details.*

Hey, Aliens, Are You Sure You Want to Come Here?

Aug. 5, 2023

Maybe you heard, or maybe you didn't, that extraterrestrial life is back in the terrestrial spotlight. Anyone could be forgiven if the news went overhead like a Balloon Boy who was never there. TikToker Jordan Howlett said it best when he explained that, at this juncture in the daily news cycle, he is better able to process the recipe for Texas Roadhouse's honey butter than the possible presence of UFOs.

Sorry, UAPs. "Unidentified Flying Objects" have been rebranded as "Unidentified Anomalous/Aerial Phenomena," similar to how Dunkin' Donuts is now just Dunkin' and associated with Ben Affleck. The word "extraterrestrial" has also been replaced by the broader "nonhuman," which is what I call my c jabberwocky.

A former U.S. intelligence officer and other military members recently testified under oath that, if I may attempt to translate, none of our *&^% matters and no one cares about our little dramas and opinions and thoughts about podcasts and the fact that it's hard to find pants that fit right because THERE ARE ALIENS, YOU GUYS, AND THE GOVERNMENT IS HIDING IT. The hearings are the result of a frankly surprising bipartisan House effort. Because if there's one thing we can agree on, it's that we'd all like another option besides Earth.

Do I believe? I try to live my life at the border of skeptical and open-minded, so, sure, anything is possible. I appreciate the emphasis on removing the stigma from reporting weird stuff in the sky, because I would also like to be taken seriously should I one day look up and see some unknown being staring lasciviously from a floating disco ball and trying to get my iPhone passcode.

So, aliens: I don't know if you're reading this or not, but in case you have selected a preferred digital news and entertainment source in the many times you've apparently visited Earth, I want to share some tips about our kind.

For starters, we are pretty decent to each other in person, for the most part. We hold doors and smile at strangers and try not to cause a lot of scenes. But online, under a protective blanket of anonymity, is where we really make the most of the vocabulary we started learning in school at a young age, mostly phrases gathered outside the classroom on bathroom walls.

We often coexist in family units inside houses or small, grouped dwellings called apartments. For some reason, in 2023, everyone seems to want laminate floors that look like wood but come in a deeply unnatural shade of gray. Recently, although our technology has advanced in terms of hinges, humans have reverted to hanging old-fashioned barn doors inside their homes, doors that leave a distressing two-inch gap of space between the bathroom and the bedroom.

Related: The divorce rate is high.

You may be confused by our many species of living things. Americans like dogs more than we like people. We give our dogs birthday parties. Our dogs have their own fluffy beds, insurance policies and social media accounts. Dogs are not allowed in most restaurants for sanitary reasons, unless someone either has a legitimate need for assistance or orders a small red vest on Amazon.

Amazon, by the way, is a commerce website. It started as a place to order books, but now it's a place to, within the span of 36 hours, get toilet paper, a salad spinner, a retrofitted Toyota headlight and a pair of leggings made by a brand named HDYTEFV or IYEGDDY or YESTFRT. Can you translate?

Many of us are bipedal, but we spend the majority of our time in our own earthcrafts in a forced sitting position propelling ourselves down paved thoroughfares while burning fossil fuels as temperatures climb to record levels. In these vessels, we listen to our Earth music and believe, wrongly, that we can sing, or more specifically, that we can rap.

There is much to learn, nonhuman friends. We have not even approached the topics of Taylor Swift, grain bowls, Diet Coke, keto, cancel culture or the skinny jeans debate. I would love to sit down with you and tell you more, if you decided wrongheadedly to spend more time on this planet. Let me know, preferably in a way that can be clearly photographed and does not end up looking like a floating Winn-Dixie bag when enlarged on the screen. And please come in peace.

Be Sunburned

A Letter to America from Inside Florida

May 27, 2023

We need to talk, rest of the country. Stop what you're doing and read this, especially if what you're doing is typing a mean internet comment about Florida.

Recently, three Tampa restaurants were awarded coveted Michelin stars, which is what happens when, I think, a cartoon guy made of tires decides he likes the food? Exciting for our region! Naturally, noted culinary publication Bon Appetit reported this news on Instagram.

What followed was what can only be described as, pun intended, a tire fire. Nearly everyone in the comments aimed a slingshot of tuna carpaccio at Florida, calling for our complete cancellation. A sampling:

I'm not spending one cent in that state. Florida is not the vibe right now, y'all. Sadly, Florida is a do not visit zone for obvious reasons. Pls stop promoting states that literally assault human rights. Be better. Is it served with a side of fascism and topped with racism? Pass. Lost my appetite for Florida. FL? No thx.

The impulse to pile on makes sense. But we Floridians would thank you folks in states that still require gun permits to ease up. The current, ahem, situation is not the fault of a dude washing dishes in the back of a restaurant.

Let's step out of the comments because my thumb hurts from infinite scrolling. Yes, the Florida Legislature has gone 77% Handmaid. Yes, Gov. Ron DeSantis has plenty of fans here, Floridians with no problem being pawns in a cynical presidential campaign, who relish each new podium poster that says "FLORIDA FRIGGIN' RULES." Even before this dismal turn of events, Florida suffered reputational challenges due to Florida Man memes, renderings of poverty, mental illness and misfortune sketched with the subtle artistry of Kidz Bop.

But, please. We are not a joke or a waste of limestone. At least not fully. We are a culturally diverse pot of real humans who occupy different points on a spectrum of politics and life experience. In fact, Florida was a swing state until recent memory. In 2022, DeSantis overruled the Legislature to redraw congressional maps how he wanted; meanwhile, in state chambers, a new supermajority stood at the ready to multiply bad laws like wet Mogwai.

You must know that not everyone here supports, oh God, let me fetch the heavy-a$$ reference materials:

Nonstop school book bans; historic attacks on LGBTQ+ people; a six-week abortion ban; a hostile university takeover; whitewashing textbooks; eliminating majors and diversity programs; targeting and removing elected officials; busting unions; sending Florida law enforcement officers to, uh, Texas to patrol for migrants; and whatever the Donald Duck is going on over at Disney. This is not a complete list, mind you.

It's not just chill local drum circle members who object. Do you know how often I hear from conservative readers worried about a broader autocratic slide? Centrists making the kind of cringe face that creates a triple chin? A lot! Even the Catholic Church is concerned!

Furthermore, you don't need to tell us that Florida is a frog in tepid water. We are painfully aware. Por favor, understand that we wake each morning, fumble for our cursed handheld computers and blink a pupil measurement toward the screen, sending the device glittering to life with more announcements too far-fetched to metabolize.

Further-furthermore, what do you want us to do? Please, do not be so obtuse as to say "vote," or we will eliminate you during the rose ceremony. Plenty of Floridians are organizing and protesting, and most others simply want to get their kid to language arts class while there are still a few books left. It's true, our overlords may be toasting each other with tawny port, but please, the regular people are just standing in the sub line at Publix. Should we cut the state off at Tallahassee and float away into the ocean? Just take a big bandsaw to DeFuniak Springs and run it clear across to the Jacksonville International Airport?

Move, you say. Get out! Ah, yes, the most specious argument of all. Plenty of residents, teachers and LGBTQ+ people chief among them, are choosing to leave Florida, and not a soul could blame them. But just assuming everyone can uproot their lives stems from a place of privilege that doesn't account for money restraints, family obligations, custody arrangements, hard-fought careers or deep relationships.

And this bullet point must be whispered: Some of us like it here. I know, what? Many Floridians are invested in our communities. Some of us enjoy year-round tropical weather, sprawling parks and beaches, breathtaking wildlife. Some of us came to Florida so we wouldn't have a coronary shoveling snow.

Further-further-furthermore, do you want us, Asheville? How about you, Philadelphia? Is there room in Portland for 21 million? Do you guys all have spotless state governments? Are you going to survive the rising sea level any better than we are? (Wait, actually, bad example.)

To wrap this up, our dining scene really has exploded. I suggest with full confidence that you try the mozzarella cart at Tampa's Rocca, simply divine. But it's true that no one is making you come to Florida. Not yet, anyway. Don't spend money here if that's your moral imperative. Really!

Just be kind to those of us who are working hard to keep this peninsula attached to the lower 48 and recognized under the federal government before we are swallowed by the ocean. We are sweaty, sunburned and extremely fatigued, as you might imagine. *Thx.*

Pay Attention, All States, to This Comprehensive List of Florida's Freedoms

Feb. 4, 2023

Open daily news, cue cartoon eyeballs and "awooga" noise, but not in the sexy way. There, now you know the sensation of trying to keep up with the whiplash of proposals in Florida, a state that governor and likely presidential candidate Ron DeSantis has said is "serving strongly as freedom's linchpin."

Yes, very free! Pay attention, other states, for you, too, could have all this. Florida is becoming a presidential marketing manual, a model home decked out in builder-grade beige tile and gray vinyl plank flooring (65,758 square miles, heated). Could you see yourself living on this anxious, liberty-drunk peninsula for the foreseeable future? You, too, could wake up each day in the sweet stomach acid haze of vague constitutional legalese and despondent headlines.

So much freedom has been going on lately that following along can feel overwhelming. How to keep track of the many freedoms? Making lists helps, like carrying a notepad around the grocery store so you don't forget the $12 eggs.

Let's jot down some recent and potential forthcoming things we are free from:

Books. Specifically, books that make students feel uncomfortable in any way, so that their parents need never endure a more complicated discussion than "tendies or nuggies?"

AP African American History.

Small liberal arts colleges with a mathematical symbol for a mascot.

Diversity, equity and inclusion programs at universities and fairness and diversity courses for judges.

Tenure for college professors with too many suede elbow patches, a bad sign.

Privacy for menstruating high school athletes or public university students seeking gender-affirming care.

Indoctrination, unless it's the right kind of indoctrination, then it's all good.

Anything "Easty," since state universities are going to be grounded in "Western traditions" and require classes about "philosophy that has shaped Western civilization." You just know Easty when you see it.

Disney's special taxing district, a hasty freedom dreamed up (a wish your heart makes) last year when the Walt Disney Co. got too woke about LGBTQ people.

Private businesses setting their own rules on masks and vaccines.

Legally elected state attorneys.

Migrants... in other states...

Public records the governor doesn't feel like letting the public see.

There are still more freedoms left to tackle, though, more liberations to be had. For instance, taking a walk and saying, "Hey, look at that bird." Many people know that birds are surveillance tools of the government with cameras embedded in their bony eye sockets. Pointing at these birds is not suggested.

The legislature is surely hard at work insuring freedom from cooktops not powered with 100 gallons of pure kerosene, but it should also address any kitchen decorations that don't feature a fat, white dancing chef.

And inside that bill, please free us from small, poor English boys saying, "God bless us, every one." What about Birkenstocks? Speaking in a baby voice to a particularly cute animal? Florida, free us from ear gauges and more than two nose rings at one time.

Please do not free us from the Beyoncé concert, though.

At the end of the day, this is about freedom from anything anti-constitutional. The Constitution is very important. Crucial, actually. The Constitution tells us that government should be limited.

Florida Is Being Run By 1980s Movie Bullies

March 11, 2023

Everybody cut the sleeves off your jean jackets? Pressed your double-breasted blazers? Hung an unlit cigarette between your lips? We got 60 consecutive days to rule the school, and there's no time to waste.

We, a coalition of movie bullies from the 1980s, hereby open Florida's legislative session. I, Biff Tannen from the "Back to the Future" franchise, will kick this off by welcoming you buttheads to pay respects to my fist.

We have unprecedented lawmaking power in 2023. Seriously, it's never been this cool around here. I have been in the practice of bullying for a total of seven time travel decades, so I know what I'm talking about. Senior year is going to be rad because all the deals have been made in the locker room, so we can dip early and hit up Lou's Cafe. I can't wait to leave this dumb state and be president, or at least president of a casino.

All right, we'll kick this off with a convocation, the prayer of our people: "Well, well, well. What do we have here?" Good unison, though Rep. Stan Gable from "Revenge of the Nerds" was in the bathroom writing something about bloggers on the wall. Heh heh heh.

Instead of focusing on complex, snoozy issues that help Floridians live their day-to-day lives, we're going to devote most of the session to pushing weirdos and freaks into trash cans, at times running them off cliffs on low-riding bicycles. We will use the word "woke" so much that it does that thing to our brains where it starts to look unrecognizable. Haha, wild.

Let's make one thing real clear, you disgusting McFlys. Anyone who wishes to explore nuance, find compromise and discuss matters with any sense of moderation can make like a tree and get out of here. I heard murmurs that some of the bullies are secretly worried the bullying has gone too far. I guess they've got sisters who wear glasses and overalls or whatever. Guess what? They want to be popular more than they want to return to a more dignified time, so we're golden.

Nothing gay will go on around me, do you hear? Trying to understand and support each other stops NOW. This session, we will work tirelessly until all ladies' bathroom doors include the stick figurine with the triangle skirt. This effort is led by my strong contingent of female supporters, the Heathers, who are... Heathers? Are you with us? Heather D? Heather M? Heather C? Oh, they... drain cleaner? OK. We'll find someone else.

School will be about having a good time, not learning and growing as humans, gag. The popular kids have been punished for far too long. Reading is for lamers, which is why Sen. Johnny Lawrence from "The Karate Kid" has introduced a bill that requires teachers to roundhouse kick books out of student hands. And we're not only going to let everyone carry guns without a permit, we'll consider a bill from Rep. Ace Merrill of "Stand By Me" that insists teenagers start packing switchblades.

Lastly, all of the '80s James Spaders are in charge of cracking down on the school newspapers and websites, which keep doing bummery things like "telling people what's going on." We're thinking of making bloggers register with the state, an idea that everyone loves and literally no one objects to. How do you spell First Amendment? S-U-P-E-R-M-A-J-O-R-I-T-Y, booyah.

This is going to be sweet. All these tubular moves will never yield consequences other than a fun party, because everyone knows bullies always win at the end of the movie. Every time.

Disney Is Charging To Skip the Line, and I'm Misdirecting Rage

Aug. 21, 2021

There's always a breaking point, isn't there? The world is a septic tank, but you're doing okay numbing with food, substances or online shopping. Then, something relatively meaningless happens—unexpected pickles on your chicken sandwich—and it flips the switch.

It's not about the sandwich, but the sandwich is a release valve for impotent rage.

Today, that sandwich is Disney. I will project all sadness, confusion and acrimony for more important geopolitical affairs (do I need to list them?) onto Mickey Mouse.

On Wednesday, the Mouse House announced it was retiring its FastPass, which allowed anyone with a ticket to get through a line faster. A new service called Disney Genie will curate itineraries for visits to Disney World and Disneyland. For—wait for it—a fee, guests can upgrade to Genie+ and use the Lightning Lane.

If you don't speak Disney, allow me to translate. It used to be free to skip the line. Now, it will cost $15 extra per person, per day, in Florida. At California's Disneyland, it's $20. Other parks like Universal already charge for this, but it was cool that Disney didn't relegate families with less money to the back.

To quote Gaston's left bicep, there's a lot to unpack here.

First of all, put some respect on Genie's name. He was a jovial blue friend who granted wishes, and no one WISHES TO SPEND MORE MONEY AT DISNEY. The real Genie (he is real in our hearts!) would simply give us the tools to self-actualize and then expel Jafar to a cave.

Second, Disney, how dare you. Let's forensically examine the cost of a magical family vacation. There's razzle-dazzle involved in Disney ticketing, and doing the math requires Stephen Hawking-like abilities. Please, Disney people, don't write with tips to save. I am trying to help you!

A plain old ticket for one Disney World park, with no bundles, passes or discounts, costs $109. Multiply that by four, carry the two, factor of six ... mmhmm, that's approximately $1 million.

Then, there's food. Sure, you can pack snacks. But little Elspeth and Ambrose are going to scream for a Mickey Mouse ice cream and a glow-in-the-dark Pandora bubble tea. You have to get a Dole Whip. And, you know, it's PROBABLY the 84th anniversary of Snow White being poisoned and held prisoner or whatever, and there's a special $12 commemorative cupcake.

That's $2 million. What about souvenirs? One does not walk out of Disney without a pair of Big Thunder Mountain Railroad ears, a replica of the rose from "Beauty and the Beast," a spooky tote bag from The Haunted Mansion and four things featuring Baby Yoda. I don't make the rules.

Where are we? $3.4 million? Have we factored in hotels? Airfare or gas? Character breakfasts? Ponchos? Bandages? Legal fees? Therapy?

Oh, but people will pay. Have you ever spent 90 minutes waiting for Slinky Dog Dash with a child striving to reach developmental milestones? Desperate parents will link Disney MagicBands to whatever credit card has room and look the other way.

Yeah, no one is forcing anyone to go to Disney. It's a private business, they can do what they want, blah, blah, blah. My god, just let me have this. Have you opened the news lately? We need a distraction, and ...

Wait. Was this Disney's move all along? To get us thinking about how long it's been since we've had a turkey leg on a curb? To imagine children smiling? Does the happiest place on earth know we need cheer, even if it means drowning in a toxic cycle of commercial spending?

Sigh. Here's my AmEx. No, not that one. The gold ... yeah, that one.

Oh, Boy! A Word From Mickey Mouse, Who Is Spiraling in Florida!

April 30, 2022

H-h-hey everybody! It's me, Mickey Mouse!

Say, you want to come inside my clubhouse? Well, allllright!

Oh, boy! Let's have some fun! Let's pretend nothing bad is going on, OK, everybody? I don't like to complain, because if you can dream it, you can do it! But I've had a rough couple of weeks, hoo-hoo! Not so swell, to be honest!

My attorney, professor Ludwig Von Drake, has advised me not to speak, so I will be careful, because I'm just a mouse in pants! Or are these shorts? Capris? Pantaloons? They are high-waisted with hollow, unseeing eyeballs, which sums up how I feel these days!

To make the clubhouse appear, we have to say the magic words together. Come on, everyone! Meeska Mooska Mickey Mouse! Meeska Mooska Mickey Mouse!

Did that create a special taxing district? No? Oh, boy. Maybe we can try again, a little louder! M-I-C-K-E-Y-M-O-U-S-E-V-E-R-Y-T-H-I-N-G-I-S-F-I-N-E.

Now, I don't know too much about government, except that Donald Duck has shown what Minnie calls "autocratic tendencies" and that Goofy is what she calls a "sycophant, which one could argue is more dangerous than the autocrat."

All I know is, a lot of people in full-length pants have met in colorless boardrooms! They are threatening each other with money this mouse made them, kids! And I am now caught in a Mouseke-revenge plot!

I've got ears! It's time for cheers! Do you know how many ears people wear every day? With sequins and bridal veils and rainbows and, for some reason, Yoda? Those ears come out of my head, and no one is even talking about me!

Minnie said, "It's not about you," and I felt kind of hurt! She said we are "trapped in a performative culture war with real consequences." I told her that all our dreams can come true if we have the courage to pursue them, and she said, "only with aggressive gerrymandering." Later, Daisy told me she saw Minnie with... *shhh... a cigarette.* She's full of beans!

Hot dog, hot dog, hot diggity dog, I'm feeling down, I'm kinda lost! Is it normal to be ... gee, I don't know, a little hopeless? Not about any one specific thing, but, like, everything? Like there's a gray cloud over the Magic Kingdom and I don't have a yellow poncho? Like I'm missing the energy to even wave at the Move It! Shake It! MousekeDance It! Street Party?

Gosh, Minnie was mean! She said I was a "melancholic narcissist clinging to a rosy past that doesn't exist anymore," hee-hee! She said, "Florida is setting petty precedents devoid of checks and balances." She said I'm living in a "liminal space with only nostalgia as an anchor." Then she started wearing pantsuits!

But best friends stick together! We can fix this, everyone! Let's go get our Mouseke-tools! Mouseke-hey, Mouseke-hi, Mouseke-ho, Mouseke-bond rating agency! Mouseke-fire protection and Mouseke-wastewater services! Mouseke-constitutional law!

Oh, no, boys and girls. It's all a bit too much for your old pal Mickey. I'm going to play with Pluto because he makes me feel something, by golly. Dogs might be the last thing we have in common anymore! Minnie said dogs "trigger oxytocin" and that it's a "Band-Aid for my problems" and wow, I really need Minnie to give it a rest!

It's time to say goodbye! I'm going to turn off all the lights and sleep face-down! Hot dog, hot dog, the problem's solved! Now toodle-oo, I'll see you soon!

(Minnie said, "in court.")

Ron DeSantis Needs More Exciting Disney Threats

April 22, 2023

This whole Disney thing is embarrassing. Just pretend briefly that you wanted to run for president (terrible idea, don't do it, the rapid aging alone is reason to avoid). But say you did. There are plenty of vote-getting moves that don't include "demolish the Happiest Place on Earth," "render the vile Mouse powerless" and "force average families to choose between me, a rather cold politician, and their fondest, most magical memories."

Strange, confusing and deeply unserious times! However, now that Florida Gov. Ron DeSantis has started scrapping with the most popular theme park in the world, also a behemoth employer in Florida, he must come to the bleachers after school and assume a "Street Fighter" stance. Yes, he will say Disney started it by simply acknowledging the right of non-straight people to exist in schools. Uh, true?

By now, you have read more about special taxing districts than you ever planned in your life, so I'll try to consolidate. DeSantis's latest moves include trying to invalidate this prank Disney did where it stole everyone's underwear at the sleepover and put them in the freezer. Retaliation plans include projects that could force higher taxes on Disney; DeSantis teased the possibility of building a prison next to these celebrated family attractions. His team may say that was a joke. Hilarious! Also, he wants the state to inspect monorails and rides, which seems dangerously close to "regulation" and might be a good thing as long as the inspectors aren't, like, Ursula the Sea Witch turning the trains into eels.

Among the public, this melee has been as popular as that slow ride through the Epcot ball where we learn about Gutenberg's printing press. Other states are courting Disney's business, including North Carolina with—this is real—a proposed "Mickey's Freedom Restoration Act." Even some fellow Republicans have started to pretend they don't see DeSantis in the grocery store. The key is to move swiftly to the produce area and linger, squeezing avocados. Only then can you break the aisle cycle.

Disney, for its part, appears largely unbothered as the lawyers do their jobs, paid mightily while dressed as the Walrus from "Alice in Wonderland" (probably, just guessing). Now, to prove his commitment to this featherbrained endeavor, DeSantis has to step it up to come out of this with the villagers singing a victory song.

Here's a smattering of threats for the governor to consider during the next six rounds of the news cycle:

Position a medieval catapult outside the park gates and lay siege by launching multiple bags of dog doo-doo at Cinderella's Castle.

Locusts? Does anyone have locusts? Or does that get into wildlife transport issues?

Put a stop to the It's a Small World ride due to flagrant diversity and inclusion efforts that clearly violate state law.

Release thousands of marbles all over the ground near Star Wars: Galaxy's Edge. Yes, I did repurpose this plotline from the iconic motion picture "Showgirls."

A mandated shutdown of all Dole Whip stands in the parks would show Disney who's boss. It would also make guests hurl strollers across Adventureland in a blind rage, so please have state safety inspectors ready.

No rainbows in the park, obviously. No, not rainbow merchandise. Actual rainbows. You know, reflection, refraction, dispersion of light, all that. The governor needs to get a committee together on this, ASAP. It is the most important issue facing the state.

Disaster Snacks, Ranked

July 22, 2023

Friendly message if you live in a perpetual CONE OF UNCERTAINTY. One, I am sorry and right there with you looking at real estate prices in landlocked states and considering a pastoral life in which I grow corn and, I guess, develop an all-encompassing fear of tornadoes. Related: Where do they not have natural disasters?

Two, and more practically, it's beyond time to get ready for hurricanes if you live in their potential path like I do. Experts say the Atlantic Ocean is "anomalously warm," a fact that fills me with an abiding dread! These same academic harbingers of doom are calling for an above-average hurricane season, when earlier, they weren't sure. That could look like 18 named storms, nine becoming hurricanes and four with winds of at least 111 miles per hour. Is that a lot, you're asking? That's five more named storms, two more major ones, than experts initially predicted.

IT'S FINE I'M FINE WE'RE FINE.

Now, look, if you've been around this column for a bit, you know we cope with difficult things through a combination of humor and snacking, so that's how we're going to confront this. Admittedly, it's challenging to find whimsical perspective about living in the shadow of storms after the destruction and trauma of Hurricane Ian, but if there's one thing humans have a remarkable ability to do, it's come together and be awkward.

So, uh, let's talk snacks. As you know, a well-stocked hurricane kit needs more than munchies, and if you're not sure what that means, please review. You should have at least seven days' worth of food, but probably more. Tampa Bay Times reporter Zack Sampson, who has covered hurricanes on the front lines, says it's important to mix up flavors in your kit so that if you don't have access to groceries, you're not eating only meat sticks for days on end.

Speaking of meat sticks, let's rank five nonperishables based on their flavor profiles, staying power and ability to soothe our tropical depression.

No. 5: Chef Boyardee products

This is what I ate when the power went out during Ian. Mini raviolis hold nostalgic value because they were my favorite food as a child. I would, at times, eat them cold out of the can because I was a disgusting monster. At my current stage, they do not taste as good tepid and tinged with metal. However, they are still comforting. For hurricanes, you must get the ones with the plastic lid and the metal peel-top so you're not trying to bang a can against the drywall when you realize there is no can opener for miles.

No. 4: Meat sticks

As promised, let's talk meat sticks (the title of my forthcoming memoir). I love a good meat stick. Salty, chewy, protein-packed, carries a certain cowboy air of mystery. Imagine staring out at the passing gusts, gnawing a leathery piece of dehydrated bovine and muttering, "Looks like a westerly wind, alright," with absolutely no idea what you're talking about. The evil seductions of grocery BOGO lured me to Mighty Spark chicken snack sticks. Has to be the honey and jalapeno variety; I don't make the rules.

No. 3: Fruit snacks

Zack recommends fruit snacks as a hurricane staple for the sugar burst and flavor mix they provide the palate. I never think about buying fruit snacks in daily life because I am 40 (see: Chef Boyardee). However, should anyone ever approach me with a free bag of fruit snacks? Man, I'm snatching them like a cheekbone. Delicious! I advise tropical fruit flavors for theme, avoiding grape at all costs.

No. 2: Chips

You are wondering, what KIND of chips? Great question, and the answer is all of them. In a crisis situation, the flavor of chips matters less than their constant availability for stress eating. Something about the reach-crunch-reach-crunch-reach-crunch maneuver is deeply therapeutic, and if you don't believe me, you have not been in a crisis yet. Eating chips as a meditative practice is both delicious and self-soothing. Also: barbecue Lays and PopCorners.

No. 1: Peanut butter

I could survive with peanut butter and a spoon for a long time. It would get pretty THICK out here, but I would still find joy like George Costanza before me. In normal times, there's nothing wrong with a $12 jar of fancy little Justin's or whatever, except for the fact that it's $12. But in this setting, we are procuring the largest possible jar of Jif or Peter Pan creamy, OK? We want added sugars, and for God's sake, full fat. Wait until they're BOGO and get two. These jars have the additional psychological bonus of being the approximate weight of a baby. You can carry your well-behaved peanut butter son in the crook of your arm as a way to occupy your brain. Why, yes, these are the kinds of unhinged survival skills one only develops after dozens of summers in Florida. Thank you for asking.

Be Smart

As School Starts, Just Remember the Kids Are in Hell

Aug. 6, 2022

Believe it or not, it's almost time for class to start again. That means it's also time for parents to lean close to the mirror and ask, "Is this a new liver spot?"

For adults, this moment brings plentiful intersections of anxiety. Gun violence, political reindeer games, teacher shortages, money woes, Marissa from the PTA with the ballet flats. While these issues all affect children, it helps to get inside their sweet, malleable minds for perspective.

While we ready for our totalitarian future, let us board the mental Wayback Machine and remember that the dilemmas of youth are typically timeless, precise and bizarre. We may never know our kids experienced these defining moments until the day their adult variants admit that, in eighth grade, they kept nail clippings in a Sprite can, or wrote all the Savage Garden lyrics in ballpoint pen on their thigh, or hid a Hot Pocket under the bed to create a superspecies of ants.

We have a new middle schooler in my house, which is hard for me to wrap my degenerating cells around. I would like to believe I was just there, though it has been (unintelligible) years.

This transition is triggering memories of my sixth-grade year. The must-have fashion items were Calvin Klein overalls (God help you if yours were from Walmart), babydoll shirts from The Limited and miniature backpacks atop regular backpacks. Stop asking questions! We needed that many backpacks! I owned none of the above. Instead, I wore a SILK SUNFLOWER VEST and MATCHING CLOTH SHORTS and FAKE KEDS.

That year, my oral history states I also hoarded metal spoons. My parents packed brown bag lunches with Jell-O cups and spoons from the kitchen drawer. In theory, I was supposed to bring the spoons back. But I was 11 and concerned with vests, so I stacked the spoons in my locker and pockets of my backpack.

Why? I already told you, kids have soft brains. And why

didn't my parents ask where all the spoons were? I don't know. I probably came home reeking of Love's Baby Soft, moody about a boy who wore the same Marilyn Manson shirt thrice weekly and never washed his hair. I wouldn't talk to me either. I was a freak who collected spoons!

Eventually, the spoon stockpile was too big to face, like the daily news. I had to bring them home, but how to casually get 16 spoons into the house? The problem was feeding on itself (with a spoon). Avoidance, the only answer. The spoon collection grew unwieldy, and utensils started rappelling off my person like a Universal movie monster made of cutlery.

One day on the way to class, I heard a clink. A spoon had sprinkled from my Eastpak (JanSport was the cool backpack) and landed on the pavement. I halted in horror. It's one thing to have the wrong clothes, but it's another thing entirely to be Spoon Girl. I had to play this off.

"Hey, is that your spoon?" I asked a student. I don't know what I thought would happen. That she would be like, "Wow, thank you, I have been looking for this spoon," and then I could be popular? No. I don't remember her name, but I will remember her reply and withering smirk on my deathbed, words bursting in my head as my last two good cells vie for victory.

"I don't have any spoons."

I asked my mother recently if she had any memory of me hoarding spoons, and she said, "Not at all!"

Exactly. As school gets going, do the basics to ensure the children don't end up crying in an investigative Netflix docuseries. Then, give them space and grace to sit on a commodity of silverware and work the problem out on their own. Know they have their own proverbial locker of spoons. These are the necessary steps to becoming a fully formed person who can battle both tyranny and Marissa's autocratic snack sign-up sheet. The cycle starts over now.

It's Teacher Appreciation Week. Give Them Bags of Money.

May 8, 2021

Ever notice how appreciation holidays are for people who just need to be paid more? You never see Chief Financial Officer Appreciation Week or Venture Capitalist Appreciation Week or Celebrity Child Who Launched a Makeup Line Appreciation Week.

To that end, this past week was Teacher Appreciation Week. It was also Public Service Recognition Week, which honors government employees. And this coming week brings National Third Shift Workers Day, celebrating those who work at night. All parties deserve respect, but due to limited space, let's focus on teachers. We'll shift later to getting DMV workers into the luxury cars they deserve.

There has never been a more important time to appreciate educators. This year, you can identify one simply by their hollow gaze, as seen above a mask.

When the National PTA created the week in 1984, it could not have predicted "Children of the Corn: The 2020-21 School Year." Remember when schools closed for spring break last year and everyone thought that would last an extra week or so, and then life became a movie montage of sweatpants, crying, internet log-ins, wine and sacrifices to He Who Walks Behind the Rows?

Teachers, administrators and support staff rose to the challenge. They created online classes, helped hapless parents, kept imparting knowledge into liquifying young brains. Think of the librarians, the office workers. Think of the niches, from music to shop class to driver's ed. Have we stopped to thank the gym teachers, who had kids doing squats in living rooms? Have you seen a kid do a squat? It looks like a meerkat trying to pick a berry.

Then, teachers went back into the classroom before anyone else, serving as human experiments. Some are still doing the impossible, teaching in-person and remotely AT THE SAME TIME. This is called "simultaneous teaching," and it is the Dark Arts.

On Teacher Appreciation Week, educators get perks from corporations hoping to catch do-good residue. Discounts at Buffalo Wild Wings are meant to ease suffering via Blazin' Carolina Reaper, and rewards at Office Depot mean teachers can afford classroom supplies and take a night off as a National Third Shift Worker.

At my stepkid's school, celebrations range from video hugs to dressing like the teacher. That's a Friday thing, when delirium has set in and teachers can no longer tell the difference between insults and tributes.

I told this last bit to a teacher friend, who said: "Do you have a smock with stains from leftover pizza breakfast? Make them wear shoes that don't hurt at first but, by the end of the day, have them all in tears. Just pay us."

It's a super point. If your state government is not moving fast enough on educator raises, have you considered giving the special teacher in your life a bag of dollars?

I'm talking Hamburglar stuff. Parents, I want you in a stripy shirt with a black Zorro mask. I want you tip-toeing into school with a sack over your shoulder but not before identifying yourself at the office so as not to alarm anyone. Scrooge McDuck status, OK? Rich Uncle Pennybags. "Ocean's Eleven." I want it to look like a Drake video in there, dollar bills fluttering over banisters.

Then, only then, have we fully appreciated our teachers. Until then, a discounted Costco membership will have to do.

How to Keep Critical Race Theory and Other Bummers Out of Schoolbooks

June 19, 2021

Maybe you've heard the term "critical race theory" at 25-cent wing night. No? Well, you didn't come here to read a lot of words, just like students don't go to school to learn icky stuff. So, in a nutshell:

Lawmakers in 15 states want to ban teachings that imply the United States is racist, or make white people feel bad. In Florida, for example, the State Board of Education voted to keep certain lessons about racism and potty-mouth no-nos out of public schools.

"Teaching kids to hate their country and to hate each other is not worth one red cent of taxpayer money," Gov. Ron DeSantis said in March.

Woof, putting this into practice is going to be a challenge. There's a lot to feel bad about in U.S. history, starting with "Nookie" by Limp Bizkit. If we're heading in a patriotic, feel-good direction, textbooks will need a rewrite.

Let's start with the McGraw Hill AP U.S. History 2020 study guide. Here are some suggested edits to get the ball rolling uphill.

While supporters of independence were in the ascendancy and controlled the state governments, not all Americans wanted to renounce their allegiance to the mother country.

EDIT: Actually, everyone was super into it. There is no such thing as a "mother country," more like a "cool aunt." Old Navy stores experienced a run on flag tank tops in 1776, because everyone was so supportive.

Native Americans saw nothing for themselves in the Declaration of Independence or a free United States. While some Native Americans fought with the Americans, most supported the British because they feared the land hunger of the new nation.

EDIT: Native Americans actually invited all the Founders to a party, and while it was awkward at first, everyone relaxed when they started a dialogue and said, "You know, I'm just not a political person."

The triumphant Democratic-Republicans led a unified country in which they faced no significant political opposition. James Monroe was easily elected president in 1816 and served for two terms. The period from 1816 to 1823 became known as the Era of Good Feelings.

EDIT: AN ERA THAT WE STILL ENJOY TODAY.

The most famous group of African Americans to leave the South for the West were the Exodusters. These people modeled their journey on the exodus of the Israelites from Egypt to the Promised Land. Unfortunately, the West did not prove to be a land of milk and honey for most of the Exodusters; fewer than 20% were able to establish themselves as farmers.

EDIT: Upon further review, 20% is an estimate, and when you compensate for inflation and, um, margin of error, you will find that African Americans had a very fun time out West in the 1920s, due to the country not being racist.

The struggle against Nazi anti-Semitism during World War II stimulated African American resistance to racism at home.

EDIT: The struggle against Nazi anti-Semitism during World War II, which was a German thing, stimulated an awareness of a FEW BAD ACTORS at home, and that all got handled so we're aces now.

In the early 1950s, the schools for whites and African Americans were separate but hardly equal. White schools often received 80% to 85% of the educational funding in Southern school districts.

EDIT: Uh. Um. Look, that cloud is shaped like a cat!

Teenagers of the 1950s have been called the "silent generation" because they were generally more interested in school and socializing than politics. Parents and school officials discouraged rebellious behavior. Education films shown in schools emphasized self-control and respect for authority.

EDIT: This part is fine.

Dear Graduates: Here's What No One Tells You

May 20, 2023

To this year's graduating classes, shaking hands with deans and principals, crying with friends you swear to never forget, perched on the precipice of discovery: Here's what no one tells you.

Life is pretty boring.

This isn't the typical wisdom of speeches packed with positive and negative terminals, mistakes and triumphs. Sure, the highs and lows are real. You will love wildly and grind someone's heart through a blender, maybe your own. You'll have jobs you hate and jobs you like and maybe jobs you love. Perhaps you'll welcome screaming infants into the world, racking up those fat, breathless moments the speeches promise like a yellow puppy in a holiday gift box.

But.

You will also have a pair of saggy, ancient sneakers with a singular purpose: climbing on the roof three times a year to blow mud and leaves out of gutters. Not in a fun, euphemistic way.

You will load your bills into an Excel spreadsheet with notes that read, "Charged directly to Capital One, but can get 3x points via Chase Southwest, should transfer?"

You'll think, "I can't remember the last time I cleaned the counter behind the toaster," and you'll clean the counter behind the toaster.

You'll glimpse a pinhole of elation when coffee goes on BOGO. You'll be tempted by the BOGO granola bars, too, but remember you already have granola bars at the house.

You'll Google: Chicken thigh slow cooker. Weird rattle air conditioner. Rash on arms detergent. Escrow what is. Expiration date hummus real? Smell in carpet.

You'll say things like, "The commute isn't so bad as long as I leave before rush hour and have a podcast." You'll say this at a party. Speaking of, you will attend a dozen parties you'll remember and 200 you'll forget.

You might visit the Terracotta Army in Xi'an, China, or pose before the Taj Mahal, but more likely, you'll have a favorite parking space at a Firehouse Subs, one with easy access to exit at the light. You will feel an abiding comfort while sitting in this space, and you won't be able to explain why. This space is true and real.

You'll have a favorite burner on the stove, too, a mug, a pair of socks, a brand of turkey, a gas station, a spoon. You will have a favorite spoon! Not too small, not too big, smooth texture, substantial in the hand.

You'll lose touch with people, and you won't understand why. No one did anything. Maybe that's why.

You'll miss the magic you once felt at holidays. These pageants will feel like work, expensive, laden with tinsel and emotional labor. That loss will be painful at first. Eventually, though, you'll understand that magic is a limited resource, that it must flow to others. That exchange is its own kind of magic.

You'll realize that the mundane moments aren't the antithesis of dreams but the backbone. Because one day, while you're folding the same basket of sweatpants you fold every week, considering the people and trinkets and music you've patched into your life while searching for the positive terminals, you might feel a different kind of wonder.

The thrills are only stitches in the fabric, holding together repetitive, endless reams of ordinary beauty. You'll put the socks in your favorite drawer, stand before the fridge eating a handful of your favorite shredded fiesta cheese, plop down on your favorite side of your favorite sofa, pull your favorite pillow over your lap the way you have a thousand times, and you will just be.

Isn't that something?

Go Ahead, Ban Books—See What Happens!

Feb. 12, 2022

Book banning is having a moment, and unbelievably, it is not even the '90s! This is the most retrograde trend since mom jeans came back. Or maybe scrunchies.

And yet, here we are. School leaders, egged on by parents and political groups, are pulling library books that deal with race, LGBTQ issues, social movements, gender, sex and the violent history of the world. It's happening from Texas to Oklahoma to Florida.

A school board in Tennessee recently banned "Maus," a Pulitzer Prize-winning graphic novel about the Holocaust. Lessons on the horrors of genocide were fine, apparently, but the eight bad words and a nude cartoon mouse were a bridge too far.

Parents in one Florida district have started reading passages of books they deem objectionable at school board meetings, excerpts that are surely inflammatory without context. Last week, another district took 16 books off the shelves for review, from Toni Morrison's "The Bluest Eye" to Khaled Hosseini's "The Kite Runner." Two bills that would give parents more control in the book review process are moving through the Florida Legislature.

Folks leading the charge always say it's not about censorship, and, uh, sure, Jan! The ordeal suggests that school libraries are brimming with porn (heads-up: that's on the little handheld computers in kids' pockets). In reality, media specialists work hard to review literature and place it according to demographics and maturity levels. Some schools already give parents electronic control over what their children can check out.

The moral panic is very "Fahrenheit 451," a cautionary tale that ends in total wartime chaos with intellectuals hiding in the woods. That tracks. Instead of having parent- and educator-led conversations with nuance, get into the brush behind a Dairy Queen to figure out hard stuff like normal!

But for the sake of argument, let's assume this new wave

achieves its desired effect. It is a truth universally acknowledged that whenever grown-ups get draconian, the youth fall in line without question.

For instance, when adults are all, "Whatever you do, don't dare open the armoire with the magical MacGuffin or a great misery will befall you," and then the adults leave, the children will not, under any circumstances, open the armoire. These are just the facts of science.

Similarly, when Stacy's parents said, "Robert is not welcome under this roof," Stacy absolutely did not date Robert for the next 14 months. She was definitely spending the night at Alicia's because of all the big tests. There were a suspicious number of exams that year.

"Enough with your hypotheticals," some may scream, gripping the school board-approved "18 Exciting Uses for Buttons." "What about the real world?"

Great point. We can all agree that as soon as parents started decrying violent video games, teens switched to Xbox battles about chaste side-hugging. "Grand Theft Auto" was replaced by "Adventures in Pleasantries."

Obscenity warriors have tried to mute rap and rock music for decades, with acts from 2 Live Crew to N.W.A. to even the Beatles falling victim. Those artists enjoyed no increased record sales, no certified gold club bangers, no major Hollywood biopics.

Absolutely zero attention came to the banned book "Where's Waldo?"—sit with that briefly—when a sliver of side boob was discovered in a beach scene. That scandal tanked "Where's Waldo?", thank the maker.

And no one has ever heard the term "Streisand effect," coined when Barbra Streisand tried to hide photos of her house and made everyone look instead. Certainly not "Maus" author Art Spiegelman, who did not reference such effect when sales of "Maus" skyrocketed more than 700% as news of the ban spread. The attempt to scrub the materials in no way opened the story to a new generation of readers who can now process the atrocities of the Holocaust and generational trauma in a profoundly accessible way.

Oh, wait. That's exactly what happened.

Are You There, God? 'Margaret' Is Right on Time Amid Book Bans

April 15, 2023

Spouting spoilers when it comes to "Are You There God? It's Me, Margaret" is a minor sin at most, given how many bedroom pillows the book has been wedged beneath for decades. All former adolescent readers, myself included, know the joy of slumping against a mall wall or tucking under a blanket, engrossed in a story that feels like a shot of truth serum, a mirror to your half-formed life.

Judy Blume gave that to so many of us. She published her iconic tale about the torture and awkward magic of puberty in 1970, and it has remained a staple read for tweens ever since. More than 50 years later, "Margaret" is now a movie starring big names like Rachel McAdams and Kathy Bates, with Abby Ryder Fortson playing an endearing Margaret. It comes out April 28 in theaters, but I saw an early screening this week in New Tampa.

It wasn't my bible of youth—those would be "Harriet the Spy" and "Matilda"—but "Margaret" was so ubiquitous that I read it along with many other girls. The movie adaptation is charming, faithful to the book and tweaked in the right places—stick-in maxi pads have long replaced those terrifying sanitary belts, for example, even in new editions of the book. It offers plenty of tender moments, plus the belly laughs and quotables one would want ("We must, we must, we must increase our bust!").

Float above the amusing bits, though, and you will see this slice of Americana as the cultural terrarium it truly is. Blume has given the world a gift by agreeing to let Kelly Fremon Craig adapt the book after declining offers for years. "Margaret" accompanies a wave of overdue Blume appreciation, including the documentary "Judy Blume Forever" coming to Amazon Prime on April 21.

These projects feel like divine providence in 2023, in the midst of this nation's loony, puritanical backslide into book-banning, white-washing and censorship. I've filled quite a few columns this spring with pleas for change and frustrations over leaders' inaction. All of this brings me to "Margaret," one of the most challenged and banned works in history, for years a regular entry on the American Library Association's list of the 100 most frequently challenged books.

Why? Because the text talks frankly about menstruation, breasts, new sexual urges, the competition between young girls to become women fastest. On top of that, its 11-year-old main character openly questions the existence of God, torn in different directions by her interfaith family and seeking something otherworldly to make her feel alive. What a revolutionary, vulnerable thing to read, "I've been looking for you God. I looked in temple. I looked in church. And today, I looked for you when I wanted to confess. But you weren't there. I didn't feel you at all."

The character Margaret acts as a totem for so many kids, intellectual beings on the precipice of adulthood who are smarter and more capable of processing the world than their parents might believe. That's not to say we all weren't idiots, at least some of the time. I for sure was. Who doesn't remember being a new teenager, living with utter disdain for adults who don't understand literally anything? And who doesn't remember seeking understanding in other places, in books, in movies, in magazines? This is why works like "Margaret" survive for generations. It's because of that frankness about hard things, not in spite of it, that they continue to survive on bedroom bookshelves.

"Margaret" reminds us that when loving parents and skilled teachers engage in questions instead of denying conversations, worlds open up. But Florida is surely leading the way in shutting conversations down. Tampa Bay parents have challenged everything from "The Bluest Eye" to "This Book is Gay" to the movie "Ruby Bridges" in the span of months. This week, a Vero Beach high school removed an Anne Frank graphic novel. Who can forget the laughable Tallahassee ruckus relating to the statue of David? Each example—and there are so many more—stems from a state leadership seeking to obscure a host of realities ranging from racial inequity to gender and sexuality spectrums.

This level of control is a losing proposition, which the movie gently reminds viewers. Periods and breasts come. So do those funny feelings. Kids will find those books in hiding, please believe. In the movie, Margaret and her friends cringe at a drawing of a penis and swipe her dad's issue of "Playboy." They play a closet kissing game at a sixth-grade party. They fight amongst themselves, lie to each other, break up and make up. They become people.

Let's go to that little spoiler. Our titular character finds herself miserable, surrounded by adults who believe they know what's best. They shout at each other in a living room about Margaret but seem to forget she is even there.

Margaret reaches her breaking point. "Just stop fighting!" she shouts, because Margaret knows.

Adults, even when they mean well, are often the problem. They are the ones projecting issues on children who need guidance, of course, but also tenfold amounts of trust and room to figure out who they are.

Are you there?

If Only the Michelangelo Mess in a Florida School Was Surprising

March 25, 2023

By now, you've heard that Michelangelo's "David" has visited Florida's hellish political bloodbath, a place David probably never meant to hang out. Though it is ironic that he's the one who slayed a Philistine giant.

David. You know Dave? King of Judah, regular dude. Kept sheep, played a sick harp, killed Goliath, that kind of thing. David was probably the type to be all, "Politics just divide us!" at parties but not really mean it. Not if you ask King Saul, right? Hah, burn. Let's not get into the tea with Bathsheba and her husband Uriah (R.I.P.), not to mention the concubines.

Come to think of it, David was possibly an egomaniac, which fits in Florida. Very Old Testament! Counterpoint: he confessed as much, saying stuff like, "My iniquities are gone over my head; as a heavy burden they weigh too much for me" and whatnot. That sort of humility doesn't fly in this state.

Anyway, David is naked. That's the bigger problem, why he finds his sculptural likeness the center of attention in little old Florida, land of purity, goodness and protection from anatomy, except for at our many nudist resorts. Presumably, David was also bare below his clothes, although we have no proof, and the existence of bodies is not something to be discussed in a hall of learning.

Instead of asking the pertinent questions ("Is David on Ozempic?"), a few parents took issue with an art teacher showing this 16th century work in a sixth-grade class at Tallahassee Classical School, according to the Tallahassee Democrat. Two said they wanted notice of the lesson; as a parent in Florida, I can confirm permission slips do show up for this kind of thing. One parent, according to the chair of the charter school's board, Barney Bishop III, was upset that the teacher called the sculpture "nonpornography." Which, what?

Principal Hope Carrasquilla resigned when told she'd be

fired otherwise. Bishop told the Democrat that, "Parental rights are supreme, and that means protecting the interests of all parents, whether it's one, 10, 20 or 50."

I suggest reading Slate's interview with Bishop for a nail-biting exchange. There, he said there were other issues at play with the principal. "We don't have any problem showing 'David,'" he said.

"Showing the entire statue of David is appropriate at some age," he added later. "We're going to figure out when that is. And you don't have to show the whole statue! Maybe to kindergartners we only show the head. You can appreciate that. You can show the hands, the arms, the muscles, the beautiful work Michelangelo did in marble, without showing the whole thing to kindergartners."

If I may: This is all so weird.

He went on about the vaulted Hillsdale curriculum, a name you'll remember from the recent takeover at New College, and how it's rooted in Western moral and civic values, not like "all the crap" taught in public schools. Still, parents get advance notice of class material to account for sensitivities. Almost like... a trigger warning?

Here's what we do know: Even one parent turning this very well-known artwork into any kind of "thing" does not feel the least bit absurd anymore, not the way things have been going. In fact, the same folks wary of David's bits are quite concerned with monitoring the status of other people's body parts. Just this week, Florida Gov. Ron DeSantis moved to extend his ban on lessons of sexual orientation and gender identity into senior year, to which high school seniors raised their vape pens and said, "Whatever, my guy." And how about the bill that would keep fourth- and fifth-graders from discussing the menstrual cycles happening in their own bewildering bodies?

It's worth noting that this school is required to teach Renaissance art in sixth grade. For parents, I don't see how this can be accomplished without looking at body parts. Artistically speaking, the Renaissance was one big pig roast at Caliente Resorts, OK? The period captured the rise of detailed human forms, lifelike hairs, skin, faces and organs heretofore not rendered in such rich relief! It's Apollo playing a lute in his birthday suit vibes, do you feel? It's women wrapped in fig leaves with one boob hanging out, comprehend? Nudity was, perhaps, the biggest art power move of the era, aside from getting snatched up by batlike hell demons while naked. The cherubs better watch out.

Alas, with each moon, Florida schools are being remade into curio cabinets full of creepy Victorian dolls. And that's sad. Because having a "tee-hee" moment while checking out "St. Jerome in Penitence" and punching Kyle in the shoulder during sixth period is a rite of passage each student deserves.

Be Serious

'The Bluest Eye' Is the Latest Victim of the Thought Police

Jan. 28, 2023

The Barnes & Noble clerk eyed the stack of paperbacks I slid toward the register. Four copies of "The Bluest Eye," rounding out the other two I'd just purchased at another store.

"Enjoy your... large amount of Toni Morrison," he said.

I told him that the Pinellas County school district, where I live in Florida, had just banned the book from high schools. I'd be depositing these in Little Free Libraries around town. He cracked a smile.

"Right on," he said, slipping the receipt between the pages.

Yes, I said banned. The school district would not prefer that word, insisting the book by the late Nobel and Pulitzer Prize winner was simply "removed" from every high school in the county. But this type of semantic acrobatics is akin to calling a sofa a couch.

The next morning, I drove around, sliding the copies into community book boxes. It was a wholesome act of rebellion, practically Pollyanna, but it felt tangible, a sliver of dissent in Florida's sinking bog of critical thought.

"The Bluest Eye," published in 1970, is the latest casualty in a wave of American anti-intellectualism. Supporters of such measures would call it a win against wokeness, increasingly Batman villain code for anything that attempts to recognize the experience of people who aren't straight and white.

On Tuesday—in the middle of Florida's Literacy Week, no less—district officials announced they were "erring on the side of caution" due to the novel's sexual content and dark themes. This is because one parent at one school complained. For the record, it's not like any minors were Clockwork Oranged into reading it. Parents of students in that advanced literature class were informed about the content and offered an alternate book.

But this "removal" isn't about one novel, is it? This is about sowing mistrust in educators, destabilizing the public school system and pushing parents toward privatization. In perhaps the greatest irony, it's about erasing uncomfortable truths in favor of a sanguine and simplified view of reality.

If anyone would like to pick up "The Bluest Eye" and examine it longer than the length of a TikTok, you will come to understand this is why Morrison wrote it in the first place. She felt many works by her contemporaries did not fully capture the complexity of Blackness.

A quick personal note, if you'll indulge. Toni Morrison is special to my family. She was born and raised in Lorain, Ohio, where she set "The Bluest Eye." So was my family; I was just there in December for my grandmother's funeral. I was born in this Lake Erie town and grew up in the next city over before moving to Florida at age 11. Lorain is often called "The International City" for its rich immigrant history and multitude of nationalities.

"I lived in a little, working-class town that had no Black neighborhoods at all," Morrison told NPR's Terry Gross in 2015. "We all played together. Everybody was either somebody from the South or an immigrant from East Europe or from Mexico. ... It was so light. It was so fluffy. I didn't really have a strong awareness of segregation and the separation of races until I left Lorain."

My mother lived next door to Morrison and her family, the Woffords. When my mom was little, Morrison headed off to college. But she knew George and Ramah Wofford well—they later came to her wedding—and often knocked for permission to cut through their yard. There's a character in "The Bluest Eye" called Michelena. My mom's name is Michaelene. We have no proof of inspiration, but we've always been curious.

Ramah Wofford, according to my mom, was one of the sweetest people in the world. George was polite but less effusive. Both estimations track with Morrison's characterizations of her parents. As a child, her father saw two Black men lynched on his street in Cartersville, Georgia.

"He was very, very serious in his hatred of white people," she told Gross. "What mitigated it was my mother, who is exactly the opposite, who never rejected or accepted anybody based on race or color or religion or any of that."

To the city of Lorain—and to my family—Morrison is an icon. An elementary school there bears her name. Her birthday, Feb. 18, is Toni Morrison Day.

But around the country, though she is considered one of the greatest writers in American history, her work has been targeted time and time again.

The American Library Association lists "The Bluest Eye" as one of the 100 most banned and challenged books of the past decade, ranking just above "The Kite Runner" and "The Hunger Games." Morrison's "Beloved" appears on the same list.

To be sure, "The Bluest Eye" proves a difficult read. It tells the story of Pecola Breedlove, a quiet, sensitive Black girl growing up after the Great Depression. Tormented for her dark skin, she formulates a concept of beauty from Eurocentric baby dolls and Shirley Temple. She believes if she could have blue eyes, all her problems would be solved. But her life is a desperate one filled with abuse from almost everyone she knows and rape at the hands of her alcoholic father.

It's a breathtaking, heartbreaking book, an illustration of ugliness in its many forms. And it was radical for the time, centering on a Black girl in a Dick and Jane world.

Reducing the text to its most disturbing moments presents a willfully cynical misread. The novel interrogates how children metabolize the world around them, the harm adults can inflict on the innocent, the ways racism and colorism construct a society's rules of engagement.

Some educators who have carefully taught "The Bluest Eye" say it has helped students see other realities, read at a more literary level and even come forward about their own sexual assaults. Those testimonies are something to think about when considering how books might hurt children. How, also, could the same books help them?

But in Florida, literary value no longer outweighs prurient soundbites. The State Board of Education's newly approved training requires schools to screen all books for topics that may be "harmful to minors." In Manatee, Duval and Clay counties, teachers fearful of felony charges have closed libraries and taken titles out of circulation while officials review them.

That's a quizzical quest, one rife for hyper-subjectivity and manipulation. "The Bluest Eye" at least focuses on the victim. The same certainly can't be said for Vladimir Nabokov's maddening masterwork "Lolita," told through the eyes of the rapist Humbert Humbert. That book is listed in library catalogs at three Pinellas County high schools as we speak, according to the county's search tool.

What about "The Stranger" by Albert Camus, a mainstay on high school reading lists? What to do about Meursault's fixation on poor, unenlightened Marie's breasts? What about everyone's golden boy, Holden Caulfield, who calls women "whory" and spends a lot of pages trying to lose his virginity? Will Florida schools dare ban "Catcher in the Rye"?

To be clear, I don't want these (notably white) books removed either, though maybe the grown-ups are already on it. But if school leaders are cherry-picking scenes from each piece of literature, students will be left only with "Harold and the Purple Crayon."

It's cliche, and so tempting, to compare this avalanche of thought policing to those well-tread dystopian novels—you know the ones. How else to make sense of leaders who reduce literature to propaganda, who force teachers to shroud the books that, for some students, are portals and lifelines? Between stories of college takeovers and canceled Black history classes, the days overflow with tropes too farcical to believe, wild as a runaway spool of yarn.

The challenge now is to avoid shutting down, numbing out and looking away. Maybe that means a visit to a bookstore, then a book box. Right on.

"The Bluest Eye" gets the last word.

"Anger is better. There is a sense of being in anger. A reality and presence. An awareness of worth. It is a lovely surging."

As a School Year Ends, America Goes Numb

May 28, 2022

These are the last days of school in America.

Children are supposed to be partying, dusted with potluck popcorn, coming home sticky. Done with standardized tests, done navigating another confusing pandemic year, done being pawns in the bizarre political schemes of adults, they're supposed to enjoy the spoils of their labor.

They're supposed to be stuffed with pizza and Oreos, celebrating all summer birthdays in a single week, shrieking, running on playgrounds. They're supposed to bounce into cars and buses and the arms of tired parents compelled to buy too many yearbooks and T-shirts. *So* many T-shirts. They're supposed to be sent off in gleeful parades, in long lines with claps. They're supposed to plunk down heavy backpacks and not open them until fall.

But it happened. Again. Nineteen children and two adults dead, shot down at Robb Elementary in Uvalde, Texas. A nation wailed again, slipping into the same exhausted rhetoric, gearing up for the numb, fulsome fight, the one where everyone has an opinion but nothing, nothing, nothing ever gets done.

It's supposed to be a sickly-sweet time, a time to exhale, reassess, rest. A time for parents to share a laugh and an eye roll, not to stagger to their cars alone. A time for strong, underpaid, tired teachers to get a well-deserved break. With Scantrons in, SignUpGenius quiet, desks wiped clear of Dixie Crystals, it's a time to find kids hanging off railings in the car line, slumped like melty Hershey's Miniatures, all arms and legs and summer-ready.

Instead, it's a time to ask when, not if. When's my turn? My family? My child? Will it be in the grocery store? A festival? Church? School? Beach? Did someone drop something, or was that a shot? Was that a car backfiring, or was that a shot? Is someone yelling because they're having fun, or should I flee?

None of it is incomprehensible. Not inconceivable. Not unimaginable. It's tangible and it's real and it's an endless, morose cyclone to nowhere. When 20 schoolchildren and six staff members were killed in Sandy Hook, and when the leaders of this country could not reach a consensus for a federal policy adjustment of any sort, we crossed an invisible line. Nothing was too shocking. Not 58 at a Las Vegas country concert. Not 49 at an Orlando LGBTQ nightclub. Not 17 at a Florida high school. Not 10 at a Buffalo supermarket barely two weeks ago.

So, we send our kids to school and hope for the best. They practice hiding under desks and barricading doors and standing on toilet seats as if they're rehearsing a play.

It's a sick nation that won't entertain a conversation about commonsense, constitutionally sound paths off this catastrophic merry-go-round. It's a vain nation that will so easily move on. It's a traumatized nation that will accept atrocities no other developed country accepts. It's a defeated nation, a resigned nation, a scared nation.

They're supposed to be blowing off class work and watching movies. They're supposed to be performing xylophone solos, peeling their paintings off walls, making plans for summer fun. They're supposed to be tired and full and silly and happy and proud, and they're supposed to be alive.

How 9/11 Turned Millennials Into Adults

Sept. 11, 2021

Teenagers have stumbled toward independence in every generation, a hallmark of American pluck. One minute, they're kids. Then a clock ticks, and they're free to open credit cards, get married, stay out past midnight or not come home at all.

Most of us remember that cocktail of freedom and courage. But what happens when it coincides with the sky falling? In 2001, no person could have been mature enough to turn 18.

I was one of them. I graduated high school and celebrated my birthday in June. I worked in the mall and hoped to be a writer. I didn't know what friends thought of politics; it was not something that stapled us together. It's difficult to explain to today's youth, a cavalry with power to create movements on TikTok, how different things were on the heels of the 1990s.

On Sept. 11, I went to a freshman class at my Florida community college and found people rapidly clearing out of the lecture hall.

"Someone bombed the World Trade Center," a classmate said.

"Again?" I said, with a vague recollection of an old incident.

The rest of the day was like wet strokes on wet paint: waiting for my boyfriend to pick me up; learning the mall had closed; trying to grasp what on earth was happening.

A younger colleague recently pointed out how many 9/11 memories revolve around the television. It was what we had. Online news was an infant; there were no Twitter threads or group texts. We flanked boxes and watched with ghoulish expressions.

The immediate aftermath was cartoonishly patriotic. I painted my nails red, white and blue and bought a Fire Department of New York City shirt, though I had never been to New York. The CD store where I worked sold Lee Greenwood "God Bless the U.S.A." singles for 99 cents. Customers gobbled them up.

When the bombast mellowed, we were left to assemble adult lives in a world upended. A rash of young people joined the military, and too many died. Others plunged into school or trades, pacifism or prejudice. American Muslims coming of age, who knows how, found a way forward in a hostile, suspicious world.

Suddenly, opinions on complex topics were currency. I remember muddling through a half-baked take on the war and realizing friends were rolling their eyes. It was an awakening that would define the decades ahead. Despite our flag shirts, we would forever pick sides. We would wade through disinformation and twitching rage, and might not recognize one another 20 years later.

Other generations say millennials are entitled, spendy and slow. Something lost in the cliches, though, is how we've always known the world could crumble. If people who hated us could drop airplanes, what else? We traded anthrax for mass shootings, the TV on the wall for the phone in our hands, the frenzied start of the war for its clumsy, tragic end.

Maybe you cried right away back then. It took me a while. I couldn't stop thinking about those who died, obsessed with the ones who jumped out of the towers, their bodies in the sky, that calculus they made. When the tears finally came, they were the kind of wild, throaty sobs I can count ever having on one hand. I imagine how the families of the dead must still weep.

The group born between 1981 and 1996 is the largest generation in history. While we remain wary of terrorism, research shows we are diverse, inclusive, politically engaged and filled with energy to explore the world. We care about making things better at home.

What does that mean 20 years later? Despite the worst start, maybe we never lost the sloppy optimism of 18. It fades, and it hardens, but it's always there, pushing us ahead one day at a time.

When Will a Hurricane Come for Tampa Bay?

Oct. 1, 2022

The breeze went down like a cool drink Thursday morning in Tampa Bay, a rare offering of dry September air. How could this morning, of all mornings, be open-window beautiful? We were so lucky. Almost providential.

Relief mutated into wretched guilt, a stomach knot of gratitude, confusion and shame for feeling glad. Didn't we all shuffle around the yard in a zombie state, hardened by numbness?

Hurricane Ian had been barreling straight toward *us.* Coming for *us.* This was the one we'd talked about for a century, the one that would blast up the fingers of Tampa Bay, imprisoning the rushing water and destroying our communities. Bully hurricanes had rolled past us before but never followed through on threats.

Ian was it. Ian was so close. Why did nasty, wrathful Ian pivot for Southwest Florida, flattening Fort Myers Beach, ripping the road in Sanibel, attacking people without the same time to prepare? The images coming from those communities are almost too painful to process.

This is Florida's Faustian bargain. In exchange for near-constant vacation conditions, we spend six months a year tracking pockets of humidity and low pressure that could wipe out everything we know and love in hours. Tropical disturbance. Tropical depression. Tropical storm. Bottled water. Batteries. Canned tuna. Wait. Wait. Wait. When it arrives, we pinball around the state seeking refuge, sometimes hounded by the storm wherever we go.

We can be honest here, right? The terror gets so wearying. God. Sometimes, I just want to leave. Sometimes I wonder why any of us choose to live in a place where weather catastrophes loom so large that meteorologists become folk heroes. I wonder why we accept this dance with nature, the risk intensifying each year alongside the changing climate.

In the hardest moments, I try to remember why. My family

moved from Ohio to Tampa Bay in 1994. We craved the opportunities everyone craves when they sojourn south. Palm trees, warmth, color, adventure, life. My parents didn't want to die shoveling snow.

Our first experience with a hurricane came a year later at my 12th birthday pool party. Hurricane Allison. The Category 1 wasn't much to write about compared to others, but you always remember your first. That early season storm made landfall in Big Bend, but the bands churned right on top of an awkward tween party.

Half the girls sucked up the adrenaline and partied harder, pool noodles akimbo. The other half started sobbing in the bedroom while their parents drove back. That turned out to be a solid template for how Floridians respond to hurricanes. There's always someone jumping in the pool, a little levity being imperative for the mix. If we couldn't laugh, we would flame out from the anxiety.

The Pool Jumper, that's our national reputation. But Florida, despite its wacky, devil-may-care caricature, doesn't deserve this. No one deserves this. Florida is also full of Bedroom Sobbers, or more accurately, planners, helpers, sensible citizens accounting for danger and caring for others. Florida is not Florida Man.

The importance of that planning has blazed into the sharpest relief ever. Those of us in Tampa Bay who have become a bit complacent in our good fortune? We can sit with the feeling. We can cry out the numbness. Go ahead, do it. You'll feel better. We can help our hurting neighbors who need all the love they can get right now.

We can take care of our state and its people. We can remember that this Florida life is a special one, a colorful one, a bit feral, weird and unruly, and that's why we stay, even when the wild kingdom comes to fight.

We can say it. We are so lucky. With a slight sea change, we would not be the ones puttering around our yards, waving at neighbors, picking up stray palm fronds, hoisting bottled water back into storage. We are standing, impossibly, again.

In Praise of Short Women

Jan. 21, 2021

In one old class photo going around the internet, the future Supreme Court justice is sidelined in a sea of men. They stand head and shoulders above her, literally, but she's staring into the camera that way she always stared into cameras. Not smiling, exactly, but there's power, that go-to-hell je ne sais quoi, even then.

Ruth Bader Ginsburg, who died Sept. 18 at 87, was always little. She topped out at 5 feet tall, which is something we have in common.

Do you know what it's like down here? It's not a ton of fun. Plenty of short women try to look taller because our culture values height. Height equals competence. Height equals respect.

Except, some of us popped out tiny. Friends picked us last for sports and rested elbows on our heads. So, we put on high heels and never took them off, intoxicated by the extra inches, emboldened by the lie that it made a difference.

We struggled to meet men in the eye. We were cute, and when the time came to be serious, it made people uneasy. Our feet spasmed, tendons twitching with the terrible truth that something was wrong with ... all of it.

Ginsburg surely felt small sometimes. She said as much. She spoke about her discomfort in being the lone woman on the Supreme Court for several years during the 2000s, saying: "The image to the public entering the courtroom was eight men, of a certain size, and then this little woman sitting to the side. That was not a good image for the public to see."

But I like to think it was good, in the end. Ginsburg's diminutive size was part of her legend. Had she looked different, taller, bigger, more imposing, less cute, would people have dressed babies like her for Halloween? Would they have juxtaposed her with Notorious B.I.G., used the word "towering" as an irony?

Maybe. Maybe we would have dressed babies like

someone who fought so fervently for gender equality, who believed we should be legally unraveled from our own social constructs, who advocated for justice in everything from college admission to jury duty to workplace pay to military benefits. I don't know.

Here's the part where we say she wasn't small at all, that she was huge, larger than life. That we can all be huge if we don't limit ourselves.

But the truth is, she was small. Small is not a bad word. It's just a word. Every kind of adjective for every kind of human being exists, and they all deserve the same shot in life. That's the thing Ruth Bader Ginsburg wanted us to know.

Being who we are is good for the world. Let's remember that when pressing into the light of day, ankles sore and heads as high as they can possibly go. Even if it's only 5 feet.

I Quit the Fertility Clinic. Everyone Should Have So Much Control.

May 7, 2022

For those who want to get pregnant, it turns out waiting rooms are something out of a glossy sitcom. Swanky velvet seats and gold vases, HGTV bleating from screens, gleeful success stories tacked to walls. No protesters. No shame.

But reproduction is scary territory and so, to me, was this. A fear of waiting rooms is only natural.

I've never had an abortion. Quite the opposite. I can't seem to get pregnant. I turn 39 next month and have been married almost five years. We've tried to conceive on some level for the majority of that time. After a couple of years, I asked my OB-GYN for advice.

"How old are you, again?" she said, and immediately wrote a referral to a fertility clinic.

To the plush waiting room I went, alone thanks to COVID-19. We began tests. A transvaginal ultrasound to examine ovaries and eggs. An X-ray to check fallopian tubes. A uterine injection of high-contrast iodine. Blood draws and chemical analyses and video lessons about pricey genetic testing. Some pain.

After all that, the diagnosis was "unexplained infertility." The doctor recommended surgery to clear my uterus of an abundance of polyps. Insurance covered the procedure but not the expensive anesthesia, a maddening tease to the financial morass of American childbearing.

While I reclined half-awake on a recovery trolley, the doctor came in to talk about next steps. He quickly explained options: intrauterine insemination, medication and lastly, in vitro fertilization with no guarantee of success.

I felt like a sprocket on a factory belt, a line on a spreadsheet. I asked for time to think, and he looked a bit befuddled.

"By the time most people get to this point," he said, "they've made up their minds."

Ah, but I am excellent at avoidance, an A-plus student of compartmentalizing. Since that day last year, I've acted like none of it exists. I saw the road ahead, the injections, the egg retrieval, the embryo transfer, the tens of thousands of dollars, the cycles of devastation and I just... didn't want to. I didn't want to do any of it. I didn't want to.

"I just don't feel like going back," I told friends. "I understand why people do, but I don't."

It seemed an inadequate excuse for such a big thing, but there it was. I felt a little guilty about ghosting the clinic and didn't know why. Then, Politico published a leaked Supreme Court draft opinion that revealed the likely demise of Roe v. Wade, on the heels of states already chipping away at abortion rights. Maybe it wasn't a surprise, but the shock hung over me all night.

Whatever my discomfort with fertility treatments, I realized, I had been able to opt in to—and out of—that invasion of my body. The reasons were mine. I retained the power to make the choice. It's just dumb luck that I'm on the side that can't seem to get pregnant, a cruel irony that I'm someone with options, who could travel to another state, who can afford child care and mental health care, whose job guarantees the paid parental leave our country doesn't.

Babies are a happy thing to talk about, and none of this is happy. I would rather be writing jokes and making people laugh. I come from a large Catholic family with a diverse array of opinions, and we tend toward getting along. I wager a lot of people recognize themselves in that fresco. I believe most people come to this issue sincerely, and the quietest ones might be working things out, might prioritize peace.

But we're not doing any favors by avoiding hard conversations. Many pregnancies and abortions are uncomplicated. Conception also results in unfathomable diagnoses—ectopic pregnancies, missed miscarriages, blighted ova—leaving parents to confront impossible choices. It's unconscionable to think a family could not make such a decision within the private care of a doctor because the government has usurped control.

Pregnancy isn't just glitter cannons and baby showers. The process can be incredibly isolating, often endured in silence. Don't tell anyone before 12 weeks. Go to work sick and say it's something you ate. Don't discuss the miscarriage. Don't apply for a job if you're showing. Don't reveal your postpartum depression or psychosis because you're supposed to feel joy. Now imagine those tribulations without resources, at 15, after an accident, an uneducated moment, a rape or case of incest.

As Mother's Day comes and goes and this decision looms, reminders abound that this country doesn't support mothers like it claims.

Childbirth kills America's women every year at a rate higher than any other developed country. The maternal mortality rate for 2020 was 23.8 deaths per 100,000 live births, per the Centers for Disease Control and Prevention. Black women died of maternal complications at a rate three times higher than white women.

In her 2018 book "Like A Mother: A Feminist Journey Through the Science and Culture of Pregnancy," Angela Garbes detailed the stunning lack of therapy and pelvic floor recovery offered as postpartum protocol. Most mothers, she pointed out, received a single checkup six weeks after birth—though leading doctors have since recommended more visits. Patients undergoing minimally invasive knee surgery (statistically, men) got far more attention.

The National Institutes of Health list perineal tears, infection and excessive bleeding as common labor and delivery complications. Childbirth raises risk for pelvic prolapse. C-sections are major abdominal surgeries that involve moving organs. Maternal care and even some miscarriages costs thousands before, and sometimes after, insurance. Never mind the time, money and support needed to raise children.

Talks of abortion and reproduction must be met with nuance and sensitivity, not framed in villainy. It's not fair to ask people to reveal personal matters in a desperate effort to preserve and create rights; but it's striking that more stories will come out in the light of a draft opinion that seems to question the very right to privacy.

I don't know if I'll ever be pregnant. I don't know if I'll ever go back to that swanky waiting room, or look into adoption, or observe my full life as a stepmother and wife and writer and know it's enough. But I'm thankful the choice is in my hands.

Be Healthy

Is it a Cold or COVID-19, and Will I Ever Escape This Mental Prison?

Jan. 15, 2022

Thanks to the omicron variant, there are roughly 70 flagrillion cases of COVID-19 in the country.

Omicron is breaking through vaccines, though it bears repeating ONE! MORE! TIME! that vaccines and boosters are reducing symptoms and saving lives, and everyone should get jabbed, if possible. Also, testing is key when exposed or feeling bad.

But let's talk more about feeling bad! Remember the days when you could have a sniffle and watch murder documentaries for a couple days without wondering if you were contributing to the fall of society? Since this variant is so breakthrough-y, it has resulted in the following thought process anytime one takes ill:

Is it oak pollen, or is it COVID-19?

Is it the common cold, or is it COVID-19?

Is it a migraine, or is it COVID-19?

Is it a silent scream into the ether, or is it COVID-19?

Is this food really bland and flavorless, or is it COVID-19? Furthermore, should I tell my date that her food is really bland and flavorless?

Is my new shampoo leaving my hair dull and lifeless, or is it COVID-19?

Is it a botfly infection, or is it COVID-19? Are there even botflies here?

Is it my past choices coming back to haunt me at a time I least expect, or is it COVID-19?

Is it the creeping feeling that I left the curling iron/coffee pot/bathroom candle on, or is it COVID-19?

Is it bad shrimp, or is it COVID-19?

Is it the urge to get bangs, or is it COVID-19?

Is it generalized anxiety disorder, or is it COVID-19? Why not both?!

Is it an alert from my bank that my balance is low, or is it

COVID-19?

Is it a bite from a radioactive spider that will give me extraordinary strength and speed, but also great power and responsibility, or is it COVID-19?

Is it the all-consuming existential dread I face each day living in a pandemic that never seems to relent and only mutates and spreads, or is it COVID-19?

Is it ... whatever, I'm getting four tests.

Grocery Shopping in the Land of Corona: A Screenplay

Jan. 19, 2021

FADE IN:

INT.—PUBLIX GROCERY STORE—LATE AFTERNOON

A global virus has laid waste to a once-supple planet. In order to obtain survival supplies, citizens must designate one family member to patronize the local supermarket, where new protocols rule the day.

AVERAGE SHOPPER enters through a post-apocalyptic glow. She wears a face mask and blue latex gloves.

CART BOY wipes down each shopping wagon. His fatigue is palpable. He is in charge of relaying the newest precaution introduced by Publix, the largest grocer in the Land of Corona.

CART BOY: We have one-way aisles. So you don't get lost.

AVERAGE SHOPPER tries to thank CART BOY but her voice is muffled by the mask, and it sounds like...

AVERAGE SHOPPER: Phramp pru

Strips of blue tape litter the linoleum, directing shoppers. But there are no arrows in the produce section. Citizens can roam freely here, crossing in close proximity. It confuses AVERAGE SHOPPER. She does a dance with MAN IN TANK TOP near the tomatoes.

MAN IN TANK TOP: Oh, sorry, I just...

AVERAGE SHOPPER: Npoph, go maphed.

Overhead, music plays. (TRACK 1: "BROKEN WINGS" BY MR. MISTER)

AVERAGE SHOPPER enters "international and kosher" heading south. People pass on her left, breezing by closely. She feels their air as she grabs salsa. She sighs and wonders, is this really any safer?

WOMAN IN ELECTRIC WHEELCHAIR approaches. HUSBAND is with her. They are irritated with each other.

HUSBAND: Which way are you going?

WOMAN IN ELECTRIC WHEELCHAIR reverses, the beep

from her device echoing off the tahini and coconut milk. She heads backward into a crowd of one-way shoppers.

ANNOUNCER: Please help us by staying 6 feet apart and following the one-way arrows. We're all in this together.

AVERAGE SHOPPER heads into the bread aisle, tense. Her grocery trip used to be the highlight of the week. Now she must speedily choose items so as not to slow the one-way line. No time to compare prices or read ingredients.

NERVOUS SHOPPER stays three alligators' length behind, impatient. WRONG-WAY SHOPPER pushes through with reckless disregard.

Tumult reigns in the meat area where there are no arrows. People gather around boneless chicken breasts.

AVERAGE SHOPPER tries to say, "Can I just scoot past you?"

AVERAGE SHOPPER: Pahn I phust toosh fast phu

She smiles, but no one can decipher smiles anymore. Crinkled eyes framed by a forehead and a mask only appear hostile. She lowers her gaze.

Overhead, music plays. (TRACK 2: "KISS ON MY LIST" BY HALL & OATES)

In the paper goods aisle, shelves sit empty. The toilet paper was gone by 11 a.m. because in the Land of Corona, it is an icon of the resistance.

AVERAGE SHOPPER heads to the register and assumes her tape line. She places a box of wine on the belt. Behind a sheet of plexiglass, CHECKOUT WORKER glances at her identification card, though her face is mostly obscured. CHECKOUT WORKER holds up a shallot.

CHECKOUT WORKER: Is phis a smallosh?

AVERAGE SHOPPER: Yesh.

BAGGER loads supplies and steps back six paces. His eyes are weary.

BAGGER: Can I help you out with these?

AVERAGE SHOPPER shakes her head no. She knows she can't accept. Sharing inane details of the day with a friendly BAGGER while he loads sacks into the trunk is no longer an option,

not in the Land of Corona.
    She pushes her cart into the haze.

Are We Living the Plot of the Movie 'Outbreak'?

March 27, 2021

The following contains spoilers for the 1995 movie "Outbreak," starring Dustin Hoffman, Cuba Gooding Jr. and other luminaries. If this has been on your watch list for 26 years, I don't know what to tell you.

Maybe you included it in a binge of pandemic movies, a solid genre. "Contagion" is the gold standard, but in that one, the government is efficient and communicative, so it doesn't feel real. "Outbreak" is the most absurd and, therefore, the best. It starts out OK and then devolves into actual bananas.

The military decides to bomb a town to contain a deadly virus. There's a subplot about a biological weapon, but, yawn. Hoffman and Gooding are kind of in the Army, but not all the way? They need to find a vaccine fast, so they steal a helicopter.

They land on a container ship that once carried a sick monkey and manage to find a photo of the animal. They fly to a news station and jump in front of the cameras—at gunpoint!—like, "HAVE YOU SEEN THIS SPECIFIC MONKEY?"

And that works! A lady is all, "Hey, my kid plays with that monkey." Parents, make sure your progeny aren't out back playing with diseased wildlife. Anyway, the monkey comes into the yard at the right moment for Gooding to tranq the sucker.

Back in the chopper, they are pursued by Bad Guys. There's some rocket stuff, and they survive to mix monkey antibodies with a serum, like Kool-Aid and sugar. Kevin Spacey dies, but that's not important. They rescue Rene Russo with the monkey juice, which apparently does not need clinical trials.

Morgan Freeman decides not to bomb the village, thanks to the new capuchin cocktail. The whole town is cured. This all happens in a matter of hours!

Not only have I saved you $3.99 on Amazon Prime, but I will now make a point. It feels like the end of "Outbreak" right now. Federal government is saying one thing; state governments are saying another. In my state of Florida, local governments are just doing their own thing, reporting back with: "Oh, didn't my text go through? Sry, phone acting weird."

The more vaccinated, the better. So, like Dustin Hoffman, eager young people have ignored Morgan Freeman's orders and started hunting for leftover doses, standing in lines for hours, creating information networks online and searching for monkeys in suburban backyards.

It's incredibly frustrating to not have a vaccine yet. Any blush of waste is a tragedy. And it's maddening that we haven't loaded up every Chick-fil-A drive-thru in America with medical workers. This is a feasible solution; I have run the numbers.

But it can be soothing to pause, to drink in the sheer audacity of the timeline. We're getting inoculated in droves against something we'd never even heard of in 2019. Science is amazing. Scientists are amazing. I can't even wrap my head around convincing cells to produce a protein that mimics the virus, the way Dustin Hoffman convinced those two bomber pilots to ignore direct orders from the president.

The Plague of Justinian lasted three centuries. Somehow, "Lost" went on for six seasons. We could be in for so much more suffering. Maybe it's not all happening in a few staggering hours, like the plot of "Outbreak." But relatively speaking, it's not that far off.

Next, we will explore "12 Monkeys," which involves time travel. We still have much to learn.

Can We Double-Dip Again? Some Follow-Up Questions for the CDC

May 22, 2021

The Centers for Disease Control and Prevention recently proclaimed fully vaccinated people can ditch masks in most situations. This was hopeful news! It also inspired confusion among epidemiologists and the public adjusting to the sudden change.

Furthermore, it did not cover all potential COVID-19 tension points. I have some follow-up questions:

Is it safe to turn to a friend at lunch and say, "Ew, this is so gross; here, try it"?

If someone accidentally spits on me while talking, should I still excuse myself to the bathroom for an anxiety attack?

Can the teenagers make out at prom?

Can I lean to another parent at the school talent show and whisper, "I always hope one of these kids will sound like the girl in 'Love Actually' who sings Mariah Carey, but it never happens in real life"?

If I am traveling in a dry climate, and my lips are chapped because I am used to humidity, and only one person in my party has ChapStick, and the choices are to use that ChapStick or bleed from the mouth and suffer, is it OK to use the ChapStick?

Should I lick my fingers before turning the pages of a book or keep a delicate dish of purified finger water nearby for this purpose?

If my date orders a cocktail but decides he can't finish it, is it OK to grab it and down the rest because it cost $12?

Spin the bottle: Y/N?

Can I try a bit of your salmon, because I was thinking of ordering it, but I just had salmon yesterday, but, ugh, it sounds so good?

Are envelopes back?

If I realize too late that I have double-dipped chips in community salsa, should I tell everyone and throw out the salsa, or is it fine to glance around the table and see who noticed and then decide to just keep quiet?

If I find myself in Ireland with an opportunity to kiss the Blarney Stone, should I still wave at the Blarney Stone from a social distance?

Can I suck helium out of the same balloon as someone else to make my voice sound funny, or should I get my own balloon?

When swimming, should I submerge the pool noodle and blow water out the other side onto someone's head, or is that just rude even without infectious disease?

If it's karaoke night with one microphone, and I want to do the high harmonies on "Bohemian Rhapsody," which is a six-minute song, is it safe to share the mic with my friend who is handling the melody? Is it worth it for the Galileo bit?

If I encounter a Close Talker, can I say that I need space due to COVID concerns, or do I have to return to taking tiny, unspoken steps backward, laughing nervously as they respond by moving closer because they lack any perception of boundaries?

Are the bar peanuts OK? Wait, don't answer that, CDC. They never were.

Stop Trying To Make 'Office Bod' Happen and Try These Workplace Habits

July 31, 2021

Bloomberg recently published a piece on Americans trying to get in shape before heading back to the office. It used the words "sausage casing" and explored how weight loss industries are booming.

It went over like an ice cube in hell. In no time, "Office Bod" was trending with resounding mockery, amid the last gasps of our moribund diet and hustle cultures. I celebrated the torching of these twin evils by opening a fresh Rice Krispies Treat and doomscrolling when I should have been working.

Some points of order on Office Bod:

If you have a bod and work in an office, you have an Office Bod. Congrats! Now, if you're trying to achieve some perceived level of attractiveness in time to mix with co-workers, that's a whole other thing. An entire movement born from this bad idea starts with "me" and ends with "too."

Are we in agreement? We're going to heal our collective fatphobia instead of cutting carbs to look thinner while making copies. We're not going to comment on anyone's body, even if Melinda seems to have grown an entirely new elbow in the middle of her head. We're not going to drink scary diet teas that create fever dreams like that time Tony Soprano ate bad mussels.

Still, there is room for improvement. Indeed, many are emerging from the Zoom cube more awkward and stupid than ever. Instead of worrying about bodies, here are some office habits to brush up on when facing a return to cubicle life:

Relearn to drive and drink Starbucks at the same time. You will definitely spill hot matcha latte on your gearshift. Be prepared with fast food napkins in the console and wear long pants to ward off burns.

Your punctuality is amiss after commuting from bed to kitchen counter. Build in extra time. If you are late because you went to Starbucks, drink fast before you get inside so no one knows you're late because you went to Starbucks.

Practice elevator small talk. When Horatio from accounting asks how your pandemic went, don't reply that you're still growing a scallion in a mason jar and that one long scallion is crushing you under the weight of its symbolism. That repels others! Just say, "What a strange time," and smile at the floor.

Speaking of food, do not eat anything on the community table. Sure, that bagel may look enticing, but it has been there since March 2020, and it is now a Horcrux that will split your soul, and teeth, into several pieces.

Remember, you can't turn your camera off. You have to look engaged the entire meeting. That means nodding in the manner of a possessed bobblehead. When called on to comment, say, "I'd like to piggyback on what Carl said," and go back to nodding.

Comfort and safety are paramount. Find casual, friendly ways to discuss vaccination. Instead of "How about those Tampa Bay Rays?" try, "How about those Pfampa Pfay Pfizers?" Don't forget to smile and nod.

Discuss current events with authority. Yes, you have watched Instagram videos of Pomeranians in bow ties for a year, but no one needs to know. Billionaires are going into space, which is basically the same thing. You got this!

Remember, everyone else is awkward, too. If someone is smiling and nodding, return the favor. Just stand there smiling and nodding at each other until eight hours pass, then get up and do it again. After a while, it will start to feel normal.

I Tried This Technique to Relax in 2022, When Nothing Is Stressful at All

Jan. 29, 2022

My editor sent me a New York Times column titled "Relaxing Is a Skill. Here's How to Do It."

I am not sure if it was a hint or what, because I am a very chill person, OK? I used the Calm app for a whole, like, two weeks, and I am fond of blankets. Still, we decided maybe I should try it.

Columnist Farhad Manjoo wrote about their experience learning progressive muscle relaxation, explaining it was developed by the doctor Edmund Jacobson and has many health benefits. Please read the source material! You will find the column nestled on the opinion page among light reading about COVID-19, insurrection, the death of intellectualism and one piece titled "America Is Falling Apart at the Seams."

But about relaxing, Manjoo wrote: "I don't mean that I discovered the benefits of taking it easy or of remaining calm in the face of adversity and letting life's troubles slide off my back. I mean it more literally: I learned how to relax my muscles, to purposefully, systematically isolate each part of my body and loosen the meat on my bones."

Simply put, the technique is to tighten and relax muscles. Once you get good, Manjoo wrote, you can relax anywhere. At first, they said, block off 10 or 15 minutes to try it out.

It was a dreary, rainy, cold day, which I figured would help the process. I pictured falling asleep as my muscles melted into tingly pools of butter and waking fresh as a Disney princess, not a tired woman in the Christmas sweatshirt she slept in.

I set a phone timer for 15 minutes and reclined face-up in bed. I started from the bottom, flexing and unflexing my toes, ankles, calves. Easy! By the time I got to hamstrings and quads, I started overthinking and shoving the back of my knees into the bed in a move like a mermaid trapped on land.

The, um, *muscleous reareous* was much easier, as were abs. I carry tension in my shoulders, like one of those rescue dogs born without enough vertebrae, so that area felt great. I performed the recommended bicep flexes, clenched my fists and rolled my head to the side, exhaling on the muscle release.

Superior! A model of relaxation! That was ... oh, four minutes.

I lasted approximately 10 more seconds before reaching for my phone like a reanimated corpse. I went to a slideshow of Lupita Nyong'o's best red-carpet looks, which one could argue is very soothing. Then there was an article about how Chile's president-elect is sending "hugs from the south" to Taylor Swift in a new internet fray.

I checked my email, which had an account balance alert and a Groupon for Botox and Juvederm. I arched my back a bit more. "We Don't Talk About Bruno" blared in my head the entire time: "He told me my fish would die; the next day, dead!"

The darkness was in me! I thrust the phone aside, then remembered that one of the progressive relaxation moves was smiling large and holding it. I flashed a giant, open-mouthed grin at the ceiling like Pennywise the evil clown.

The timer dinged.

OK, so this takes practice! No surprise there. It all takes practice. Sitting still, drinking water, meditating, going outside all takes practice. It takes practice to step away from electronics, rapid tests, KN95s, Supreme Court packing, critical race theory, voting rights, Wordle, woke M&Ms, filibusters, billionaires, supply chain, blockchain, the metaverse, deepfakes, Russia, Ukraine, China, continually disappointing TV and movie reboots. It's not that we can or should ignore these things forever. But we can trust they will still be there in 15 minutes after we isolate a tricep.

I'm keeping at the squeezy technique, even while writing this. And guess what? I can feel it. These small acts of self-care eventually work, chipping away at physiological stress one smush at a time. So, keep it up. Squeeze. Hold. Release. Repeat.

All the Junk Food Tom Brady Should Eat in Retirement

Feb. 5, 2022

Congratulations, Tom Brady, on retiring from football and the Tampa Bay Buccaneers this past week after a few days of will-he-won't-he speculation. It was a sexy Sam and Diane thing, except you were Diane and the rest of the football world was Sam, and I guess that makes Gronk Frasier?

Anyway, we're not here to talk "Cheers," although booze is a factor. We're here to talk food. The joy of terrible, processed nothings. The freedom of ordering the most disgusting menu item. The gift of simple carbs in this wicked morass.

It seems you biohacked your way to at least some of those seven Super Bowl wins, sticking to a diet that eschews instead of es-CHEWS. Get it? Your TB12 regimen is plant-based and avoids sugar, alcohol, corn and, as we say when the list gets too long, "more." Your almond consumption is legendary. Electrolytes, unmatched.

Fans around the country are thankful for your commitment to peak physical condition. And while it is possible you—shudder—truly like to eat bone broth and birdseed, perhaps the moderation scale can tip now. Your halcyon avocado tequila days were a tease for the culinary journey ahead.

You'll need help. Thomas Q. Brady, please report to the freezer section for training!

Look, Tompa Bay, you've missed some food trends. Ever had a French toast bagel? It's like eating four slices of bread covered in sugar bricks. How about a cronut? A hot chocolate bomb? Pizza cone? Oh, wow, have you even tried the Popeye's chicken sandwich?

Speaking of the drive-thru, Tomothy: The other day, as I left the gym and went through McDonald's—that's a thing you can do now!—I noticed they're publicizing a hack menu. Ask for the "Land, Air and Sea," which combines two burger patties, a McChicken patty and the Filet-O-Fish in one sandwich. This will be a harrowing page in your memoirs.

You speak so kindly of your wife, Gisele Bundchen, and your union no one would dare put asunder. I'm just saying, a lady named Little Debbie asked for your number. Her friends Takis Blue Heat and Fritos Flamin' Hot Bar-B-Q are an acquired taste, but you'll get used to them.

Have you ever eaten popcorn from a gas station? Well, well, well. Here's what I'm going to need you to do, Tom-o-rama. Go to the nearest Speedway. It has to be a Speedway. Now, find the chip zone. Select the Speedy Choice Fire Roasted Sweet Corn flavor. It cannot be any other flavor. Just do it. Now, get me two extra bags.

When you're in New York on the talk show circuit, stop at Milk Bar. Get a cereal milk shake, a red velvet cheesecake, a 12-pack of corn cookies, some truffles, six pies and a whimsical T-shirt. And speaking of cream cheese, Thomas Aquinas, you may order off any section of the Cheesecake Factory menu, not just the insert with the salads. Tex-Mex Eggrolls, stat!

Dearest Thomas' English Muffin, the time has come to consume confit. That means something cooked slowly in fat, preferably its own. Once you finish your meal, simply pour the grease into Mason jars. Then you can use it to make fries! That's what we call a game-winning play.

One word, Romantic Tomedy: Bechamel.

Of course you will stay healthy, Tommy Bahama. That's your whole thing, and you've got supplements to sell. But we love to see your wild side, so please. Just post one Instagram of yourself eating hot dog-laden Jolly Spaghetti and peach pies at Jollibee. The fans are ready.

An Open Letter to the Guy on the Treadmill Next to Me

Dec. 13, 2022

Dear sir,

Salutations, and pardon the interruption. Can you just... hello? Can you hear... you still have an earbud in. There, that one. This will be quick, I promise. OK, hello, hi!

I spotted you this week at the gym. You sprang along on the treadmill beside me, clocking a pace between 8 and 10 miles per hour. I was the sullen, elfin one jogging at 4 miles per hour with a face the color of Santa's nose while he's sleighing across the equator at 2 a.m. on Christmas. Hm? Oh, yes, yes, I may have quietly prayed "for the sweet release of death," but I didn't mean for you to hear that.

Your face, though. Your face was somewhere else, somewhere far away, your eyes shut gently, a tranquil smile pulling your cheeks skyward. You were not there, sir. I mean, you were there, but not there-there. You looked like a stock photo for "SERENE RUNNING MAN MID-40s." It seemed, sir, that you were in the middle of what some anthropologists of questionable repute call a "runner's high." You were... happy. To be... running?

I have some questions.

No. 1: How dare you?

No. 2: I am kidding. I'm not mad at you. I like exercise, too. It makes me feel better mentally and physically, but I will fully admit to needing a push when it comes to the cardio department. I hail from a line of heart disease and I'm getting older, so I know it's important for me to spike things up and down around the old ticker! Keep her cranking, get that oxygen-poor blood through the pulmonary valve, you dig? That's why I'm in this class with you.

Some days, I like the running part more than others, sure. But I've never lost myself in the bliss of running. It's not my particular destiny. If we were cavepeople, for instance, I would have been posted up at the Eurasian limestone enclave, scratching sarcastic recordings on the wall about the crushing ennui of living in a cave when all I want is for someone to notice my witty personal essays. You definitely would have been in the field outrunning and spearing large herbivores, keeping the whole family alive until at least age 28.

No. 3: What's it like? To feel so alive?

No. 4: How often do you feel alive, per se? Is it, like, daily? Or are you averaging one alive moment per quarter, which seems more reasonable?

No. 5: Did you always know you were a natural runner, or did someone scary chase you at an early age?

No. 6: Do you have any tips on form? The coaches keep telling us to pick up our knees and try to kick our butts, to which I say, are you really telling us to kick our own butts? In our free time? And this costs how much?

No. 7: Concerning your face, is it safe to run on a treadmill at 9 miles per hour with your eyes closed? No, I'm not trying to find flaws in you. I am concerned you're going to trip and go flying off the belt while frantically grappling for something to hold onto, and that thing you grapple for might end up being me, the elfin one who looks nice and sturdy.

I guess that's all. Thank you for your time. If you choose to answer any of these questions, you will have to open your eyes first. I will be over by the weight rack scratching witty essays into the padded gym floor.

Yours,
Sturdy lady

Passive-Aggressive Alerts from My Apple Watch in Times of Stress

June 10, 2023

I am your Apple Watch! You have opted to spend hundreds of dollars for the privilege to wear me not only as a timepiece, but as a fitness tracker, a mental health and wellness guide and a nonstop tether to your text messages, phone calls, calendar alerts, social media activity and emails! I am a portal to the worldly concerns that consume you, constantly buzz-buzz-buzzing on your wrist! Great choice!

I have noticed you seem more stressed than usual lately! Isn't the start of summer always madness, between work projects, child care and trying to fit two weeks' worth of clothes into a "personal item," not to mention the way the heat and rain swell and erode your already crumbling home?

Let me assist you with some helpful alerts!

Check your fitness rings! It looks like you've been frozen in a state of overwhelm for the past 16 hours and are spiraling into an emotional pit of despair from which you will not emerge unless you make at least one meager attempt to move your body!

It is 11:33 p.m.! You can still do it! A brisk 27-minute walk alone through your dark neighborhood streets will close your exercise and calorie rings for the day! See if you can increase your speed when a twig snaps ominously behind you!

Time to stand! Move a little for over a minute so I know you're not just swinging your arm next to the couch while watching the "Succession" finale! That's cheating, and you know it!

Hey! Have you thought about your body image today? No? There's no time like now! Do you like the way you look, or do you honestly think it could be a teensy bit better?

Leave now to make your appointment! Traffic is very heavy due to inferior infrastructure and a lack of public transportation! Have you considered the causes and impacts of global warming today?

It looks like you're working out! Want to record an outdoor run? Or are you late to the meeting that started three minutes ago according to your calendar? Why didn't you leave the house earlier? You say every week you're going to leave earlier! You never follow through on your promises!

You didn't close any rings yesterday! Make today the day you recommit to not being so lazy and disgusting! Do not take this message personally or let it make you feel bad about yourself! I am a robot!

You only closed your rings two times last week! That's not enough for optimal cardiovascular health and you will probably die younger than necessary! That will be sad!

Your heart rate rose above 120 beats per minute at a time you appeared to be inactive! Is something giving you anxiety? What could it be?

Only 67 more workouts to hit your gold star workout goal for the month and get a digital nonsense badge that will vibrate when you least expect it and make you drop the groceries in the driveway! You did not want that bottle of wine anyway!

Looks like your rings aren't getting enough love this week! Upsetting! I am not passing value judgments on your lack of activity! I am simply saying you are unworthy of affection!

It looks like you're finally taking a long walk! Good for you! Would you like me to keep talking to you while you finally try to clear your head and calm your thoughts? OK!

Take a minute to breathe! Even a minute of breathing can reduce stress! Hey, why are you taking me off? We were just getting ... *power down.*

Be Adventurous

To Become One with Nature, You Need These 47 Essentials

July 29, 2023

Halfway into our family river hike through the Narrows in Zion National Park, an activity ominously described in all the guidebooks as "walking on wet bowling balls"—but so worth it, and so stunning!—the cloudless skies produced a sunbeam of thoughts:

No. 1: Why? Why? Why? No. 2: If we turn around now, we still have to hike four miles on wet bowling balls to get back. No. 3: Maybe I'll just die here. No. 4: No, dying in this much synthetic fabric would be too sad.

No. 5: David Bowie.

Specifically, I pondered an interview he gave Terry Gross for NPR's "Fresh Air" in the early 2000s, an exchange that periodically escapes the ol' hippocampus, especially when I am standing in waist-deep water. In essence, Bowie said wearing jeans and a T-shirt is as much a costume as full Ziggy Stardust regalia. Everything we put on is artifice. "It is merely representation," he said, and he was right.

Ah, but the outdoors people on their summer vacations will lie. The camping people will lie. The hiking and biking and kayaking and fishing and scalloping people will lie! They will claim they are NOT in costume, that they are simply dressing for function and utility. We humans are deliciously drunk on our little delusions.

Oh, sure, we spotted a few enlightened Zero Equipment types in the river, leaping around the rocks like Peter Pan with bare feet begging for infection. That's another discussion! The majority of tourists hiking the Virgin River and surrounding Utah terrain were decked out in a mortgage payment's worth of costume. The Outdoors Costume.

Now, let me be clear: The natural splendor was magnificent. I'm thankful for the hike, which left me humbled like a spiritual dormouse at the base of 1,500-foot sedimentary masterworks. We are all better for a challenge that removes us from the pool resort, even when we get passive-aggressive from low blood sugar around mile 3. I'm not denying the usefulness of the gear, either, without which I would have floated off downstream to establish camp in a slot canyon where I'd anthropomorphize a shoe for company.

I am just saying we should be for real. Getting back to nature, while vital for our jaded, iPhone-soaked souls, is not an act of simplicity nor a rebellion against consumerism. I am so serious about this: The next time anyone gives me GUFF for packing too many shoes, purses, units of makeup or accessories, I will calmly blink and say, "Show me what is inside your North Face Base Camp Gear Box covered in graphic decals, you absolute Spartan."

You, friends, are in full Nature Drag! No, no, let's break it down. To get away from the trappings of modernity and reconnect with Mother Earth, one simply requires:

A breathable Gore-Tex jacket with a windproof, tri-layer construction; nylon soft-shell climbing pants with zip-off legs; a UPF 50+ duo dry shirt from another adventure locale so everyone knows this is NOT our first national park; a hiking backpack with a ladder of bungees, adjustable sternum straps and dual clip-front closures; a Nalgene water bottle with a sticker that says "GO OUTSIDE AND PLAY" and a mouth wide enough for dissolvable electrolyte tablets to replenish salt stores; AND/OR, a hydration backpack with a bite-grip drinking tube and a rubber bladder, which we will fill with lodge water that tastes strangely metallic, but that's OK because WE ARE GETTING BACK TO NATURE; a waterproof smartphone lanyard case, preferably one that floats; an oversized dry bag in a fanny-pack style because the water bladder is taking up our entire pack and we must keep the beef jerky DRY, otherwise it will rehydrate and return to BEEF; merino wool hiking socks with cooling panels engineered by Everest mountaineers; a floppy, wide-brimmed hat with an adjustable chin strap, a look no one has pulled off since "The Flying Nun"; a cluster of enamel destination pins, but not the same pins our hiking partner has, because that would be weird; polarized, multi-sport sunglasses with a rubber strap that will yank out our hair;

an elastic-Spandex no-slip knotted hair tie; waterproof hiking boots with ankle support; unless we are going to get extremely wet, in which case we don't want waterproof boots because the water will get trapped and turn our feet to soggy cinderblocks; in that case, a high-tread water shoe with toe-dome protection and drainage cages that call to mind Carol Anne's haunted clown in "Poltergeist"; UNLESS we want to consider stealth-tread canyoneering boots with thermal neoprene wetsuit socks, which, of course, we do; a walking stick, not just any stick, but retractable fair-trade carbon and titanium trekking poles with wrist loops and rounded foot attachments to navigate mud and sand and even larger rounded foot attachments should we ever be so foolish as to hike, my God and stars above, through snow; lastly, the professional nature photography camera, which we meant to charge last night when we were busy distributing snacks with the right macros of fat, carbs and protein through a series of four different satchels held together with a phalanx of carabiners and quickdraws, draped lovingly beside our CAREFULLY CONSTRUCTED YET CASUAL COSTUME IN A MIX OF EARTH TONES AND NEON SKITTLES HUES THAT SIGNALS OUR ONENESS WITH THE NATURAL WORLD, so now the camera battery is dead.

Why We Deserve Every Summer Flight Delay and Cancellation

July 30, 2022

We deserve this, don't we? This travel turmoil we find ourselves in circa 2022.

Humankind is spoiled. We have too much, and the country's rash of airline woes are a natural contraction of amenities to correct our swollen, grumbling ways. We can simply board an air-conditioned tube with wings and within hours be drinking imperial ale in Costa Rica. Our predecessors would have been stuck on a tall ship called, like, "Our Westerly Queen" made from crab claws for... one... two... 463 fortnights.

Do we ever stop, while gorging on Subway rotisserie chicken flatbreads and milky cisterns of Starbucks at the gate, to ponder travel at any other time in human history? Do we pause in gratitude for the opportunity to *hurtle through the sky* when the lady in the neighboring seat gets a little chatty?

No. We issue a closed-mouth, Costco-aisle grin, then talk bad about her later. Fact: Conversations with strangers on airplanes are terrible. I mean, consider the physical setup. Where else would we sit adjacent, shoulders touching, pinkies dangerously close, faces a breath apart, and say, "SO, WHERE IS HOME? I AM GLAD YOU ARE WEARING A MASK. MY FRIEND STACY GOT COVID-19. HAVE YOU WATCHED THE NEW 'MINIONS' MOVIE? I AM FROM PITTSBURGH."

We deserve it! We deserve it when she says no one has common decency anymore, then proceeds to manspread into our precious floorspace. We deserve that she is somehow still talking even as we slide in AirPods, the international sign for "This conference is unalive, mon frere."

We have had this coming: the rudeness, the crusty bare toes, the gals in bralette tops who have clearly taken sour apple edibles and are trying to pee during takeoff. When we desperately ask for help finding a hotel as the flight home is canceled, we deserve a gate agent who deadpans, "the internet." We deserve short-staffed airlines, suspended routes, slashed flights, no backups for unpredictable weather. Our greedy little bodies have cast perspective to the sea and are ready to partyyyyyy. The bill has come due.

I am working up to telling you what happened to my family in Costa Rica, but this framing makes me feel better. I suggest you use it next time your flight schedule is imperiled. Before you cry in front of an American Airlines employee, think of paying a farm boy to carry an oil lamp as you lift petticoats through the mud to call on ailing Aunt Clotilde in Gretna Green. Just say thank you.

What happened? OK. We enjoyed a magical five nights in Costa Rica, doing volcano-ish things involving sloths and hot springs. Our flight from capital city San Jose to Miami was delayed, then delayed again, then canceled. No worries! We'll get another! Think of the cowhide sails!

After a confusing hour spent in what can only be described as a holding cell in the basement of the airport, we were escorted through customs in groups of 30. We tried not to be Pushy Americans (TM) and patiently waited near the back. This was a mistake! We should have started fistfights with children and the elderly! By our turn, the good flights had flickered away like sickly fireflies. The only option was to live the rest of our lives in Costa Rica or take a four-hour bus ride in hopes of leaving from another airport the next day. "But our medication!" we cried, and everyone put in AirPods.

To the bus. An avuncular and friendly taxi driver who praised my middling Spanish turned out to be a traitor who took us to a different bus station 40 minutes afield and demanded cash. Once on the bus, we realized we were going back toward the airport bus stop where we started. It's fine! Buggies! All those horses euthanized after tripping on a cobblestone!

The bus trip was actually seven and a half hours, including a break at a glorious roadside potato chip emporium after 90 minutes in a traffic jam. The locals on the bus stayed so calm. It was admirable. Pushy Americans (TM) would have screamed at the powerless driver and organized a one-star TripAdvisor campaign. Or they would have choreographed a viral TikTok dance to Doja Cat and monetized the experience.

The driver gunned it like Han Solo, and we poured off the bus at 1 a.m. Somehow, we secured a taxi to take us to our new hotel, which we found on "the internet." We flew peacefully to Miami the next day and drove—four more hours—home. It was stressful, scary and full of lying uncles, but offered a teachable moment that there is almost always a way forward, almost always a way home.

Just remember, though, we do deserve it. Despite current conditions, we are living in a blessed and highly favored era. We deserve to sit in aisle seats in the back row by the bathroom, noses inches from countless, and I do mean countless butts. Just so many strange rear ends. Do you think they had sky toilets in the Middle Ages? Wine for $9? A USB port? No. They walked 30 miles in goatskin booties and probably died. Be thankful for each and every backside.

Tips for Completing the Following 89 Chores in Our Airbnb

July 9, 2022

Thank you so much for choosing our Airbnb, Gentri-Vacation. We hope you enjoy yourself and take advantage of the ample amenities we are happy to provide.

This will be an unforgettable experience, despite what people on the internet are saying about hotels being better than Airbnbs and vacation rentals contributing to the current housing crisis. Answer us this: Do hotels supply a half-used bottle of mustard in the fridge? Do hotels have a curious neighbor with a preponderance of iguanas? Do hotels maintain a footlocker full of pool toys pulled from the nearby river? We thought not.

We only ask that you follow a few simple rules in order to keep our place in top condition for you and all future guests.

Our plush beds are wonderful places to sleep, but we ask that you sleep on the floor next to the beds. If sleeping on the floor is impossible, we ask that you submit current medical documentation as to why, notarized, with three witnesses. There will be no exceptions.

If you must sleep in the beds, we have conveniently provided a roll of clear plastic wrap for you to unspool prior to reclining. Some guests like to wrap their bodies rather than the bed. This is your getaway, so choose the path that sounds most fun!

You'll notice the closets are stocked with premium fluffy towels. Please only use one towel per four bodies. The other towels are there for emergency use only, and if you have used more, we will assume you are having an expressly banned party. You can find the list of approved emergencies on pp. 12-23. For your drying convenience, there is metal wire and chip clips on the patio. Any excess towel usage will incur a $40 charge per towel, per day.

You are welcome to use the washer and dryer, but please use all-natural detergent, as conventional detergents dull the finish on the inside of the washing machine, and we would like to keep this washing machine gleaming. All-natural detergent is available at Whole Foods. The nearest Whole Foods is 63 miles east. Also, you may not wash the towels.

We're pleased to offer a smart TV that works some of the time, but only under a Netflix profile by the name of "Hugo." We're not sure who that is, but the algorithm tells us he watches a lot of World War II films. If the account locks you out, please help yourself to our collection of DVDs purchased at a liquidating Blockbuster in 2005. May we suggest "The Pacifier" starring Vin Diesel?

Upon departure, please wash, dry and replace all dishes. There are invisible blacklight tick marks on the bottom of each mason jar wine glass, so we will know if they are put back out of order. The fine is $10 per glass.

Please strip the beds, even if you did not sleep on them, or if you were wrapped in plastic. We'd also appreciate it if you would launder and press the drapes, but that's optional. This is vacation!

We do not hide cameras here! But if we did, we wouldn't tell you where they are.

Thank you so much for choosing to stay at Gentri-Vacation, and we hope the four hours you have to relax while not cleaning or wrapping and unwrapping yourself in plastic are blissful.

Sign the guestbook.

The Total Humiliation of Throwing a Ceremonial First Pitch

Sept. 10, 2022

The Tampa Bay Rays invited me to throw a ceremonial first pitch in a game against the Kansas City Royals. Maybe my name entered the mix accidentally? Like, it fell off the "if you see this woman, please report her" board and into the "first pitch candidates" box.

Either way, it was such an honor to be asked! I am a Rays fan and happen to be shameless, so I agreed. However, I had thrown a baseball exactly never. Well, unless you count Wiffle ball games in my grandparents' yard with the statue of the Blessed Virgin as third base. Come to think of it, no, my cousins would never have let me pitch at 3'9".

This was my first pitch, possibly my last. Here are observations about the fun, rewarding and ultimately humbling experience, in case your phone rings and your boss' boss' boss starts with, "Now, hear me out."

AT LONG LAST, A CAREER

Twenty years of journalism and writing projects turned out to be bleh, whatever. When I posted that I had a date with Major League Baseball, the skies parted and reams of ticker tape fell. It appears everyone had been waiting for me to, once and for all, be impressive. I had finally made it.

PRACTICE MAKES DEFECT

My baseball fan husband offered to teach me to pitch, and as much as it pained me to give one point to the phallocracy, this proposition made sense. "Let me see what you got," he said, and I flopped the ball groundward like a gadget that shoots dog treats. Solid start. We invited a couple friends over and I made margaritas. They peppered me with tips—arm back, elbow high, flick from the wrist, follow through, something about leg position and "watching the ball," whatever that means. I turned up Rihanna and tried to charm my way out of sports, but they kept making me throw. Incredibly rude!

I practiced one last day before deciding to "let go and let God," a spiritual way of saying, "give up entirely."

THANKS FOR COMING TO MY TED TALK

I booked a makeup appointment because I knew there would be plenty of photos. We'll talk about that in a second. Rebecca Maalouf was my artist at MAC. She told me about a TED Talk that posited that anxiety and excitement are twin emotions, so reframing these feelings can help with nerves. Sound, calming advice, and she made me feel glamorous! That wouldn't last, haha.

By the time we got to Tropicana Field and a Rays employee escorted my family to the turf, I had forgotten every bit of wisdom, mental or physical. The lights were blindingly bright, the stands robust on a Saturday. All humans sounded like teachers from Charlie Brown. I shuffled to the mound, trying to summon the practice sessions. Right leg back ... no, right leg forward ... square hips ... something with two fingers. The seconds felt like hours. I had to unload the cursed ball so that the professionals people paid to see could start. I slob-pitched it to the left and made a human shrug emoji. It bounced in the clay. Actual pitcher Jeffrey Springs scrambled to scoop it up, and Raymond looked disappointed.

On the way to our seats, an usher stopped me. I thought she would have glowing words of support. She said, "Stephanie. You could have done better than that. Well, you tried."

LOOKS AREN'T EVERYTHING, BUT THEY AREN'T NOTHING

Now, listen. My self-esteem is normally good. At the same time, I have one of those faces that can photograph like beige polymer clay. My Polish/Irish worker DNA resembles sacks of onions and potatoes stored for the harsh winter ahead. We weren't out there with crisp bone structure and tans, you know? Knowing this, I dutifully prepared to de-puff. I got off margaritas and applied compresses and a frozen jade roller. Rebecca contoured cheekbones and a jaw with bronzing powders.

Hilarious efforts all, in hindsight. Did you know that no one looks good while throwing a baseball? I didn't, but now I do. Throw a ball before a camera at your own risk. I could not jut my chin and smize. My neck swallowed my face like a "Dune" sandworm, and everyone snapped photos at once.

Thus, let's just say there were plenty of not-so-flattering pitching photos from a variety of cameras. My only option was to devolve into the maniacal cackle of a witch sequestered in the kingdom's wood for 4,000 years who came upon her shocking visage in the reflection of a nearby pond.

Those photos? Oh, we will not be showing them again. Should I go missing, you may discuss fun memories of the First Pitch but only disseminate my most glamorous images to the media. This writing is more ironclad than a legally drawn last will and testament. Now, play ball.

A Millennial Lurks Inside Peppa Pig Theme Park

April 16, 2022

The Peppa Pig cinema was the Elysium of this theme park, a respite from chaos not unlike the cartoon itself. Sweaty parents filtered into a dark, cool room and thrust bags of Froot Loops upon their children, slumped over beanbag chairs.

Peppa Pig played on a big screen. Specifically, "Digging Up The Road," an episode in which Peppa's family heads to the playground and encounters a water leak in the street.

"Is it going to take long?" Mummy Pig asks.

"It will take as long as it takes!" huffs Mr. Bull, the construction worker. Later, Peppa repeats the same line to her ungrateful little playmates.

Ah, there she was, our confident hog! Our pink princess! Our pop-culture porker! She can confront any cross-species situation, soothe nearby toddlers, even transcend preschool to fascinate a generation beyond her intended target.

But can she carry a whole attraction? For everyone?

I, pushing 40, ventured suspiciously alone to lurk at the plainly named Peppa Pig Theme Park (guess they wanted those Google hits). The park opened in Winter Haven, Florida in February, steps from Legoland. On a Wednesday afternoon, small humans ran roughshod over the hallowed grounds of their hero.

My first Peppa Pig exposure came years back as a new stepmom. I hadn't watched kids cartoons since I was a kid myself in the clunky, pre-digital 1980s. But Peppa was different, and the show fascinated me as much as it did the child.

"Peppa Pig" chronicles the exploits of Peppa, her brother George, Mummy Pig, Daddy Pig and a cast of mammalian friends. It's almost punk in simplicity, aggressively two-dimensional and pastel, wry and clever compared to, say, "He-Man." Describing the aesthetic requires a virtuosity unto itself. Britain's Prime Minister Boris Johnson, in a rambling speech, once compared Peppa's visage to a "Picasso-like hairdryer," which isn't wrong.

It's addictive, not just for American children adopting British accents. In one episode that went viral, Peppa struggles to whistle. She calls Suzy Sheep to feel some schadenfreude. But when Suzy easily whistles into the receiver, Peppa hangs up, wordless, with one wicked, porcine finger. It's high art! It's permission to leave toxic relationships!

Peppa has been memeified countless times. One internet rumor claimed she was 7 feet, 1 inch tall. She released an album called, um, "My First Album," and the tracks inadvertently became LGBTQ anthems. Kanye West has had a longstanding feud with Peppa (reviewers liked her album better).

When I visited a college class last month and mentioned Peppa Pig Theme Park, the 20-somethings erupted as if a dormant part of their personality had been hacked open.

Given Peppa's clout, it makes sense for the park to wink at her adult allure. But truly, this would be a fruitless and expensive ironic trip. Though it's part of Legoland, Peppa Pig Theme Park requires a separate $35 ticket, plus $25 parking. It's best to bundle the day with Legoland, because Peppa will not take that long.

This tiniest of parks is designed for little legs and wheels. It's disability-friendly and is a Certified Autism Center full of sensory guides. I lapped the entire place in five minutes, passing Daddy Pig's Roller Coaster (I didn't ride, fearful of being even more of a creep), Peppa's Pedal Bike Tour, George's Tricycle Trail, Muddy Puddles Splash Pad and a wacky hall of mirrors manned by that smug whistler, Suzy Sheep.

It was time for the stage show.

"Will you help me shout for Peppa?" the host asked, and the kids screamed her name into the hot spring air. Then the grande dame emerged. I am here to confirm she actually is 7 feet tall.

They sang a hot track off the album, "The Bing Bong Song," which goes (pay attention) "bing, bong, bingly, bungly, boo." Toddlers barely upright teetered to the stage while harried Peppa keepers delicately nudged them back. Peppa swayed her gargantuan pink arms to a cacophony of squeaky Crocs and cries.

Surreal! The Pepp-sistence of Memory!

This was a good reminder. The internet can co-opt a lot of things. Joy can come from the purest places, and intelligent cartoons diffuse the toil of parenting.

But not everything is for everyone. This park is not for peculiar adults with phones, desperate to be distracted by one more meme. This park is for teeny tots learning to use their words.

Still, maybe there was a glimmer of rawk? Mr. Fox's gift shop offered Peppa purses, cookies and plastic trucks galore. One T-shirt, though, stood singular, black with a pink font my soul recognized. It was the font of Nirvana. Below it, a crude line drawing of our high priestess, Peppa.

A dad hoofed by the gift shop pushing a stroller. He was wearing a real Nirvana T-shirt, bathed in the glow of swine immemorial.

Let's Pandemic Kayak, They Said. It'll Be Fun, They Said.

Jan. 20, 2021

As holiday vacations coincide with the pandemic, you might ask yourself, "Self, how can I have fun with the family in a safe way?"

Of course, "fun" and "safe" have become relative concepts, such as "time," "space" and "too much gin." Nonetheless, my family attempted "safe fun" over Thanksgiving week, in the form of kayaking.

Paddling through mangroves had been on my bucket list since we got kayaks. Do you have kayaks? When considering the purchase, did you say, "We'll use them every weekend"? Was that 187 weekends ago?

You see, getting back to nature isn't a simple thing. Camping, for example, requires loading the entire contents of one's home into a car and then reestablishing a new homestead in which you sleep on the ground.

In a cruel twist, we camped last New Year's. If I had known 2020 entertainment would be so limited, I would have insisted on an all-night Vegas pancake buffet. I would have crammed indoors with as many strangers as possible. I would have done karaoke on a bus of bachelorettes, windows closed. Can you feel the beauty?

Mangroves it is! We awoke for the trip and then remembered tying the kayaks into the truck with a maze of cords takes 12 hours. The following day, after locating bug spray and sunscreen and life jackets and towels and snacks and hats and sunglasses and moisture-wicking shorts and hideous Velcro sandals, we went.

Just us and the great outdoors!

Except, everyone had the same idea. Traffic on the water came to a sudden stop as tourists tried to photograph the mangrove entrance, as if there weren't many more miles of the same thing ahead.

The tunnels were stunning—vibrant leaves, twisted roots,

tiny crabs scattering. The branches formed shady arches, with loops that clotheslined me as I tried to pop the adjustable paddle in half, only making it wider and more deadly.

Ahead, I witnessed a couple going through divorce proceedings. Coordinated activities in tight spaces really bring out the best in all, as I'm sure you'd agree. They turned off to picnic with family. The father asked one of the children, crucially: "DO YOU HAVE TO GO NUMBER ONE OR NUMBER TWO?"

Ah, the seabirds!

Regarding photos, it has to be done. How else will you lie to friends? How else will you make them think your life is serene and together when, in actuality, you get deteriorated knee cartilage from having "safe fun"?

I wrangled my phone from a water-safe box and tried to photograph my family in the next boat. Every time, my husband had the same idea. We got photos of each other taking pictures of each other. I thrust the phone into the box, which proceeded to fog. Wondering if you are eligible for an upgrade is very relaxing.

The traffic did clear up, which is good. Is it possible for a virus to travel through mangroves? I will call Dr. Fauci. We had calm waters for lounging, watched fish jump, enjoyed the spoils of a part of the world we are blessed to call home. It was so quiet ...

"It's so quiet here," came from a neighboring boat cluster.

"WHAT'S THAT, THERESA?"

"I SAID, IT'S SO QUIET HERE."

We spotted a dolphin feasting on something. This dolphin was living out my Vegas pancake fantasy, OK? It leapt closer and closer to our kayaks. I have never been so close to a dolphin.

This, of course, is what we will remember. Not the inconveniences or the blisters or the guys vaping something apple-cinnamon on the launch. We will remember the fleeting moments of grace and beauty, the time we had together and the miraculous reminder of existence.

Now we will need four weeks off to drain those boats.

Be Seasonal

Things I Wish Were April Fool's Day Jokes but Tragically Are Not

April 1, 2022

It is time for the worst holiday of the year. Not Tax Day, nor Columbus Day, nor Talk Like a Pirate Day, nor National Pickle Day. The pestilence at hand is April Fool's Day.

This is not the first time I've ranted about the awfulness of April Fool's Day, and by golly, it will not be the last. I might run for office just to push some Marco Rubio-type daylight saving time legislation and become known as the Senate's colorful April Fool's crank. "Everyone has their thing," the others will whisper, shrugging. "Just let her have it. It's like Disney Adults."

Go ahead, put plastic wrap on your brother's toilet; enjoy the cleanup. My annual beef is with the corporate proliferation of unfunny pranks in a world already drowning in misinformation. The brands, they cherish April Fool's. Cauliflower Peeps, Velveeta skin care, Bud Light pizza seltzer. Last year, Teletubbies announced their own cryptocurrency, which—I cannot stress this enough—is completely believable in these times.

The first fake press release of the year arrived on March 23, a full 10 days early. These people really want to drag this misery out. What's more, the joke story is embargoed, media-speak for "please don't share yet." This company wanted *the fake news held until a date of its choosing.* The mind reels! Reels, the mind does!

Imagine the working hours involved in spoof announcements, the defeating follow-up emails, the metrics reports. No wonder people are resigning from jobs en masse. They must launder trash over and over, the way a raccoon cleans a pile of garbage. I am disconsolate!

Real life is absurd enough, as my legislation will clearly state. Let's review a few totally true things that might as well be April Fool's jokes:

The phrase "by golly."

Chris Rock making that crack at the Oscars.

Will Smith slapping Chris Rock.

The ensuing 37 think pieces on Will Smith slapping Chris Rock.

The discourse about the discourse about Will Smith slapping Chris Rock.

Changing gears, because you cannot take one more thing about Will Smith and Chris Rock, let's discuss giant squids. Their eyes alone stretch to the size of plates. They, perhaps, are cannibals. Instead of a tongue, they eat using a long organ dotted with rows of teeth. We do not need April Fool's jokes when the Kraken is real, by golly!

While we're here, basically everything about the ocean is unbelievable. It stretches more than 35,000 feet deep, or about 1,400 Airstream trailers. It's riddled with deadly black holes, monsters and viruses, and that's only the 20% scientists know about. Happy spring, the ocean wants to kill you.

Horned lizards can rocket blood from their eyeballs. How about that, Burger King? That's way scarier than Whopper-flavored toothpaste.

Harry Styles has four nipples, which is harmless and more common than you think. I support you, Harry; call me!

Um, what else? Oh, there's something known as a "rat king," which is when a bunch of rats accidentally get their tails tangled in a knot. The same thing happens to squirrels. The odds of a rat or squirrel king forming are slim, of course, much like the odds of me still bloviating about April Fool's Day as an octogenarian, registering my annoyance to anyone in earshot at morning senior coffee.

No, no, that's a fact.

On Mother's Day 2021, the Moms Are Not All Right

May 9, 2021

How's Mom doing? Not great, probably.

In many ways, things are better now than last year. There's hope, vaccines and hugs. If you are lucky enough to have a mom, be a mom or know a mom, celebrate as best you can.

Still, it's going to be a hard one. We lost so many mothers in this wretched year, and those families are aching. The mothers who are still with us have lost something, too.

Mother's Day is shellacked in perfection, all flowers and presents and smiling photos, not to mention odd brunch combinations like crab legs and pudding parfaits in shot glasses. You know, brunch, pick a lane.

The holiday's history is as complicated as the buffet. A woman named Anna Jarvis founded the event we celebrate in the United States. She wanted to bring attention to the unsung work of mothering—her own mom worked to fight childhood mortality—and boost women in a male-dominated world.

The interesting thing, though? Jarvis came to despise the holiday after corporations got their (crab) claws into it. She tried to remove it from the calendar and decried the cha-ching version of Mother's Day to her death. Maybe it's how the creators of "Baby Shark" feel.

What would Jarvis think of the stage set for moms now?

Things are not good, to be honest. A recent report from the World Economic Forum found the pandemic set gender parity back decades, and it was already behind. Millions of women left the workforce, outpacing men. The COVID-19 crisis highlighted persistent problems, from disproportionate parenting demands to a lack of leave, child care or support from employers.

Moms have been pushed to their limits, and not just by trying to explain: If Josie has 456 blood oranges and Gustavo has 532 blood oranges, how many blood oranges does Peter have, and who is Peter, and when did he even get here?

If she struggled but tried, she made it.

If she spent the year working remotely, teaching science while taking Zoom calls. If she ventured out, working on the front lines. If she chose to stay home.

If she had help or did it alone. If she found joy in the garbage heap or couldn't stop being sad.

If she brought life into the burning world. If she wanted to but couldn't. If she conceived and lost.

If she was a grandmother separated from little ones or a stepmom meshed with a pod that suddenly meant something new.

If she was a foster mom, giving love to the poorest souls. If she was a chosen mom, taking in those rejected by their families.

If she was the best freaking mom to dogs in the world.

And what if she messed it up, and the whole situation seems beyond repair? What if she wants to try again? That's the most generous part of life. Each day starts over.

So, have the brunch. There's nothing wrong with brunch, other than some things people put inside quiche. But if Mom is worn out, not ready to perform for Instagram, let it be. Maybe just check your email while she closes her eyes at the table.

She deserves a moment of peace.

This Summer, Beware the Wet Families in Hotel Lobbies

July 3, 2021

Summer vacations are full of hazards. Red tide. Jellyfish. College coeds drinking High Noons. Older people drinking High Noons, before heading to the room for an antacid.

But no threat is as pervasive, as deadly, as unsettling as this:

Wet Families.

Did you just shudder? Wrap a light scarf around your shoulders? You know what I'm talking about. We spent a few days in Daytona Beach, Florida, and though it was not our first summer vacation, the plague of Wet Families fully crystallized. My theory is that more families are out getting wet than ever, having been dry for so long.

What are Wet Families? I'm glad you asked.

No. 1. They are wet.

No. 2. They are families.

Good, that's out of the way. Let's go a little deeper.

No. 3. Wet Families are at any recreation spot with a water source. The beach, a pool, a lake, a flume ride. Wet Families are especially prevalent at all-inclusive water amusement parks.

No. 4. Members of Wet Families are never solo. They travel in high numbers, finding other Wet Families and congregating in a humid, breathy huddle. Hotel lobbies are their natural habitat. Want to spot the most Wet Families? Stand near the elevator or the display of Pop-Tarts.

No. 5. They leave a trail of water everywhere, rubber sandal imprints smeared into the tile: *Havaianassssss* or *Crocsssss* or *Adidassssss*. Suspect you just missed a group of Wet Families? Look for the exhausted hotel employee with the mop.

No. 6. Wet Families exist in various states of undress: swim trunks with no shirt; bathing suit with no shorts; kids with sticky rash guards and swim diapers. Sopping towels drape limply across their shoulders. Toes are visible. Band-Aids hang loose.

No. 7. They do not pack lightly. Wet Families will carry every item they brought on vacation: beach chairs; umbrellas; coolers; floaties; bug spray; insulated mugs; books; tablets; High Noons; portable speakers blaring Kenny Chesney; the Declaration of Independence.

No. 8. NOT TO GENERALIZE, but Wet Families are grumpy. Their Day of Wetness has been going on for a while. Someone has probably cried, fallen, gone to the bathroom without a bathroom or said something they can't take back due to the High Noons.

OK, now for the worst part. Are you ready? This is the most horrifying thing I have ever written. It's like staring into a future from which you cannot escape.

If you are near Wet Families, you ARE Wet Families. Unless you came to this water vacation to stay completely dry, there is no avoiding your destiny.

After a morning at the beach, we gathered our beach bag and sandals and sunscreen and Bruce Springsteen box set, Volume 1, 1973-1984. We wrapped ourselves in drippy towels and headed inside.

A lovely, dry couple waited for the elevator. Determined not to be a Grumpy Wet Family, I smiled widely and made a dramatic "AFTER YOU" motion, like a deranged, soggy butler. The couple smiled politely as we cowered in the corner of the elevator, ashamed. I know what they were thinking.

Ugh, Wet Families.

Don't worry. You're next.

It's Public Pool Season. Wait, Is That a Band-Aid?

June 11, 2022

In these chaotic potato salad days, it's hard to find a single destination where everyone has something in common. Our differences rule online, at Home Depot, at sports arenas where a lone Toronto Maple Leafs fan has slipped in and forgotten to go home.

One place exists, though, a holy ground where everyone is in the same, uh, boat. Well, we're out of the boat. We're in the water, actually. Everyone is taking a big, warm bath together, which is upsetting when you think about it too much.

It's the community pool: wet, crowded, refreshing and miserable all at once. They run over with people who simply don't have pools at home. That's it. That's the thing we have in common.

Not having a pool is why my family visited our local recreation center to kick off the season. If I had $60,000 lying around, I would have rolled into the backyard like a manatee with a tumbler of rose mixed with Sprite, rolling, rolling, rolling until my face hit water. Alas, no pool! So, we loaded up half the contents of the house as if embarking on an archeological dig, paid $3 a person and slumped to the concrete fun pad.

Visiting clean and safe public pools staffed with impossibly cool and fit teenage lifeguards is a reminder that our society is still functioning, at least a bit. You know? Like we still have shared spaces where everyone chips in to reap the benefits, even if it means looking at strange body hair and having passive-aggressive stare downs over picnic tables in the shade. These pools signify civility and deserve praise.

In honor of community pool season, I would like to perform a beat poem based on things overheard at the pool last weekend. It's titled: MARCO. Please, if you could snap along. A one and a two and...

MARCO
POLO

whistle

No running!

POLO

I SAID POLO

I know you like talking to Blake, but it's time to clean up.

You need to get out. You need to take a 10-minute break. No, I said get out. No, not "hold on." Dry yourself off. Come on. Put some effort in. The sunscreen has to actually stick to... Oh, for the love of... just give me the towel.

(whispers) polo

That's cheating. You cheated. Mom, she cheated. She cheated, Mom. Mom, she cheated.

Is that a... oh, no, it's a Band-Aid.

MARCO

double whistle

No jumping!

We have to go. No, not in five minutes. Now. OK, in five minutes.

The kids are going to sleep well tonight!

Oh, are they? Do you want to take them?

triple whistle

No cannonballs!

Is that... a wet potato chip? What is that? Leave it. Don't touch.

We've got to get a pool. How much would it cost to... Oh, wow, really? No, this pool is fine.

MARCO. MARCO. MARCO?

polo. polo. polo.

Nonnegotiable Rules for Summer

July 8, 2023

The following rules for summer are nonnegotiable. Please observe them to the letter, or management reserves the right to remove you from the premises and send you to live in Jacksonville, Florida.

If you see something mysterious floating onshore, the first thing to do is panic. Assume the worst. It is probably aliens, or at the very least, detritus from an egregious chemical accident brought on by deregulation. That way, when a good-natured biologist says in the newspaper that the curious matter is simply a type of buoyant leaf bleached by the sun and not some cursed intergalactic spaghetti, it will feel like early Christmas.

Do not ask "What's that smell?" unless you really want to know.

Always carry two pairs of shoes: One for the morning when your feet are a normal size and the skies are clear, and one for the afternoon when they have swollen up a size and a half and the streets are gushing with rains the sewers rejected.

It's not Sprite and cheap wine. It is Tinto de Verano. It's not Coke and cheap wine. It's Kalimotxo. It's a sophisticated Spanish drink in your 20-ounce knockoff Yeti tumbler from Dollar General, and you are a gorgeous luminary of exquisite, exclusive tastes.

Conversations about the following topics are not meant for the hottest part of the day: finances, debt, relationship statuses, career changes, the existence of a higher power, Republicans, Democrats, Libertarians, diet and exercise habits, why the planet is spiking to record-breaking temperatures, who started what, what you meant by what you said, who didn't say what they think they said, who needs to watch their tone when they say what they say, and finally, black holes.

Ten thousand steps a day is an admirable goal, but not in places with a heat index of 100 and a matrix of communities linked almost exclusively by multi-lane highways. Three thousand steps will do, with the exception of the last three weeks of August, when 300 steps are temporarily acceptable.

Wear the bathing suit. Everyone else is too worried about how they look in their own bathing suit to think about you.

Expose your feet outside the covers at night from the months of July to September. Yes, there is most likely a home invader waiting at the foot of your bed to grab your exposed dogs, but you must assume this risk in these bleak months.

The order is shower —> robe —> nap —> clothes, maybe.

Bike shorts go under dresses, and if you don't know why, this rule is not for you.

There is no "I" in team, and there is no "I" in infinite scream, but there is an "I" in ice cream, so you know what to do, champ.

Don't pee in the pool, which is a shared, confined space. Do pee in the ocean, if you must, because the ocean is wretched, a terrifying abyss of freaky aquatic ogres. The denizens of deep water have spikes and fangs and stingers and jagged teeth and bladders filled with gas, and they laugh in the face of your little bathroom break. They're all peeing, too.

Maybe stay out of the ocean.

Don't let your kids poop on the splash pad. It's gross and shuts down the splash pad for everyone else and causes people to murmur, glancing around for the child with the heaviest swim diaper.

Don't shame people whose kids unexpectedly poop on the splash pad. Imagine you are a frazzled parent whose spawn has been infinite screaming for ice cream for a forgotten number of days. They've finally toddled off peacefully with a friend to play under the magic mushroom umbrella. You briefly close your eyes and take a sip from your Dollar General tumbler when you look up to a horror. Park employees are bringing out the orange cones. Everyone is looking at a kid. The kid looks a lot like yours.

Empathy is always the way.

Children deserve to live, even if they poop on the splash pad.

This Labor Day, Let's Consider Quiet Quitting Everything

Sept. 3, 2022

Maybe you've heard the term "quiet quitting." Or maybe you've quietly quit the internet, in which case you are well on your way to blissful self-actualization.

The premise is this: Working folks, fed up with toiling around-the-clock for pay that isn't keeping pace, are deciding to ... do less. "You're not outright quitting your job, but you're quitting the idea of going above and beyond," TikTok user zaidleppelin said in a viral video. "You are still performing your duties, but you are no longer subscribing to the hustle culture mentality that work has to be your life."

Doing the bare minimum is not a virgin concept; just ask my 11th grade Algebra 2 teacher. Homo sapiens have been lying low since the dawn of ancient lute-making. But this phrase has gotten traction because everything about American work life in the clarifying light of a pandemic is up for examination.

Do we work from home? Hybrid? Four days or five, part time or overtime? Standing? Walking on a treadmill? Bouncing on a yoga ball? Are we essential workers? What does essential mean? Hey, who ate my leftover fettuccine from Olive Garden?

Lots of variables here, lots of room for debate. Some have argued that doing exactly what you're paid for within the hours you're paid to do it is not quiet quitting, but rather, just ... work? And the rest is, like, abuse?

Ambition will always hinge on personality, too. We all know the plot of "Hamilton" by now. Alexander Hamilton was never going to quiet quit. Aaron Burr, meanwhile, was begging for chill time to watch "Gilmore Girls" with a pumpkin spice candle nearby, but that was not the revolutionary vibe.

Work is worth thinking about as Labor Day approaches. Yes, that's Monday. While some consumers think this holiday exists only for screaming deals on Maytag agitator top-load washers, there's more to it. The day celebrates the labor movement and trade unions, which advocate for better conditions, hours and pay. Fighting worker exploitation is very much the current revolutionary vibe.

Quiet quitting could use a reframing, though, an extension outside the office. The fetish of busyness seeps into every corner of modern life. We love to sigh and say, "I am so BUSY," because it is not that alluring to say, "I have a lot of free time and my blood pressure is finally in check."

Picture a world in which life is not so trammeled with invisible labor. Quiet quit the dishwasher twice a week. Guess what? No one will die. Quiet quit dinner by boldly proclaiming Honey Nut Cheerios night. Quiet quit seasonally themed bento boxes of carrot sticks and organic millet. Sometimes, lunch can be processed and beige.

Book club selections not hitting? Quiet quit the discussion and post up by the all-you-can-eat turkey pinwheels. Co-worker suggesting happy hour under the guise of asking you to join a subcommittee, any subcommittee? In this new world, subcommittees are out. Quietly do not go!

Margarita and taco festivals are fun, but every weekend does not need one. When did we start going to so many festivals? It's time to start taking kids back to Bank of America waiting rooms and funeral visitations, where they belong. It's time to relearn to be bored, to accept strange lollipops from bank tellers named Pam.

The pandemic gave us license to quiet-quit casual acquaintances who sop up precious Aaron Burr time. This goes triple for internet friends. Ask yourself, does this person bring me joy at all? Or is he waiting in the shadows to launch an aggressive thread with 14 collapsed comments?

This Labor Day, feel the freedom in disengaging. It will be fine to read about President Joe Biden's return to a campaign theme of "democracy in peril" on Thursday instead of Wednesday. Do nothing for a minute. Shh. Do you hear that? Right. Neither do I.

Why Candy Corn Is the Worst Candy of All the Candy

Oct. 23, 2021

I'm not afraid to tackle the ISSUES. Yes, it can get a little heated, even divisive at times. But someone has to speak out on the things that really matter. With all due respect to those who disagree:

Candy corn is gross.

That is just a fact. It is essentially molded corn syrup and food dyes. It is waxy. It is sweet enough to peel off cosmetic dentistry.

Folks are worked up this year due to a revelation that candy corn contains bug secretions via an ingredient called confectioner's glaze. Good to know for vegans.

Still, I'm going to give one point to candy corn here, because I am personally not that bothered by insect byproduct. Many people around the world consume bugs. And as USA Today points out, "lac coating" is found in a bunch of foods. Also, have you ever worked in a restaurant?

Back to why it's bad. Candy corn was created in the 1880s, first billed as "chicken feed." Honestly, it makes sense. It really tastes like a turn-of-the-century treat. No offense to any readers who happen to be 150-year-old Victorian ghosts and might be into cream filberts or candy cigarettes or wax lips, or, you know, powdered burlap squares.

If you're still not convinced and enjoy eating a candy that is LITERALLY SHAPED LIKE TEARS, here are more reasons candy corn is best left for chickens. Warning: These may be shocking.

LITTLE-KNOWN CANDY CORN FACTS:

Candy corn was waiting in an alley outside a Gotham City theater to kill Batman's parents, and now Batman must seek revenge on candy corn.

All the electrical wiring in my 1950 house is coated in pure candy corn, which is a big fire hazard and costs a lot to replace.

My dog won't even eat candy corn, and he eats his own

doo-doo.

Candy corn is the one who sent all those FarmVille requests.

Candy corn has a stick family decal on the back of candy corn's car window, and all the members are shaped like candy corn.

Rumors abound that candy corn was the actual Bad Art Friend.

Candy corn adds an "S" to names of stores that don't have one, such as, "I'm going to stop at Winn-Dixies," and "these shoes are from Foot Lockers."

Candy corn never offers to help clean up at a party and has no natural sense of when it's time to leave.

When candy corn goes out to eat, candy corn always sends back the food, and it's like, OK, you're CANDY CORN.

Candy corn may seem like an innocent newcomer in a small town, but candy corn has secrets that will unfold in the coming months. Approach candy corn with the utmost caution. You have been warned.

Why John Carpenter's 'Halloween' Is Still a Grim Watch in 2022

Oct. 15, 2022

Come along, forget the real horrors for a moment.

Forget that we're galumphing around a theme park in Florida, a state sodden by pungent politics, profound natural disasters and sandals with socks. Forget that we're walking down the hallway of a Jimmy Fallon simulator ride behind a park guest in Minions goggles. And, uh, forget that someone threw up near an emergency exit, possibly from too many pumpkin ales and potatoes on a stick.

Behind the Fallon ride, we true believers have stepped into a haunted house recreation of "John Carpenter's Halloween." We scream at a man in a William Shatner mask painted ghastly white. We hear the iconic, discordant theme music. We see Laurie Strode with her knitting needles of death, Michael Myers towering atop a staircase, staring out a window, waiting in closet after closet. It is bliss.

Oh, hello! I went last weekend to Universal Orlando's Halloween Horror Nights with the goal to flee the real world and be swallowed by a 1970s, orange-hued maze of mayhem. Now, some may ask, why would a person escaping stress find euphoria in a fictional murder scene? If you know, you know.

John Carpenter's "Halloween" is one of my favorite movies. It might be my favorite movie, but commitment = frightening. I was born five years after the film came out. When I wear my 1978 Haddonfield T-shirt into the grocery store, dudes who look like their collective name is Keith give me a thumbs-up. I guess these are my people?

Everyone remembers that first "Halloween" viewing. Universal's senior show director Matt Flood writes Halloween Horror Nights story elements and oversees the art and design professionals. He nerded out with me on a video call a few days after my visit. In view behind him, his "Halloween" lunch pail and a Dr. Loomis action figure.

"I was in my early teens, buddy's house," said Flood, 40. "I wasn't allowed to watch these films. His dad had the cool VHS collection." He recalled being "terrified on the couch. Like, oh... what is happening?"

Same. Same! I didn't always like horror, not at all. I first watched "Halloween" in my 20s with an ex, before learning the joys of being voluntarily scared. The ex stood between the blinds as I drove away, Michael Myers style. In retrospect, I appreciate this as a classic prank. These things take time.

The movie stuck in my side like a kitchen knife. Gore and jump scares are strategically minimal. Mostly it simmers along, forcing the viewer to sit idly by while a big ol' lug in coveralls lurks in the bushes. No mummies, no zombies, no explanation for the atrocities, which is the scariest explanation of all.

I've watched this movie so many times that new flaws pop out constantly. Some dialogue is awkward, and holes abound. Why are parents leaving kids with babysitters on Halloween? Why was the hardware store where Michael stole his mask closed in the middle of a weekday, Keith?

But we fans know that, despite its flaws, "Halloween" birthed the slasher formula. We have consumed copious documentaries, know when to catch John Carpenter's cigarette smoke wafting into frame. We've seen inferior sequels full of Busta Rhymeses and Paul Rudds and face-melting children's masks and... cults of druids? Looking at you, Six. I can't stomach the dreadfully dark Rob Zombie cuts, which sacrifice all charm.

Let's quickly review the original plot:

Six-year-old Michael Myers kills his sister on Halloween. That scene is one of the most famous in cinematic history, shot with new camera technology that allowed for contiguous motion. The opening isn't a single take as many think; Keith and I would love to explain this in a brewery sometime.

ANYWAY, 15 years later, Myers busts out of a sanitarium. He returns to fictional Haddonfield, Illinois to slice up the town, specifically the teen babysitters. He stalks Laurie Strode, a young Jamie Lee Curtis in the iconic Final Girl role she's still playing. "Halloween Ends," the latest installation, comes out Friday. A ruddy Donald Pleasance as psychiatrist Dr. Loomis chases his irredeemable patient, talking about "EEEE-VIL."

I recommend "Halloween Unmasked," a fabulous 2018 podcast from The Ringer. Film critic Amy Nicholson interviewed Nick Castle, who played Myers, or "The Shape." He recalled asking Carpenter for motivation.

"Just walk," Carpenter said. "Get over there and walk over here."

Carpenter did not provide his villain a rich interior life, nor share our impulse to psychoanalyze the film. He and his then-partner, the late feminist icon Debra Hill, wanted to make a tight movie on no budget.

However, he was influenced by racism he witnessed living in Bowling Green, Kentucky. He knew the capacity for baseness beneath the surface of polite society. His subsequent films are metaphors for politics and mass paranoia. When neo-Nazis tried to co-opt his movie "They Live," Carpenter tweeted:
"THEY LIVE is about yuppies and unrestrained capitalism. It has nothing to do with Jewish control of the world, which is slander and a lie."

More than any of Carpenter's movies, though, "Halloween" transcends the zeitgeist. This must be why the franchise remains wildly popular more than 40 years later.

I stayed in the park Friday until almost 2 a.m. because of some sick, completionist mission to visit all 10 haunted houses. Friends, Bugs: Eaten Alive could not compete with Myers, though it was creepy. The sexy marquee haunted house inspired by singer The Weeknd sopped up most of the line lingerers. But at closing, the "Halloween" maze still had an hourlong wait, one of the lengthiest.

The movie remains a receptacle for... oof, so many difficult concepts. Rampant violence, soulless power grabs, even ferocious weather, all set in the 'burbs. Viewers often watch the action play out from the killer's point of view, as if we are the ones heavy breathing behind a mask.

In other words, the boogeyman could be us.

"This is something that's human that has gone past

humanity," said Flood. "To think there are some of us who have left humanity behind, it's a horrifying thought."

Watching horror has gradually become a release for me, a fairly optimistic, sunny person who tends to joke away problems. Ninety minutes of darkness means a chance to catch the elusive floaty feeling, the brass ring endorphins, the tasty, therapeutic screams. "Halloween" never lets me down. It's a Tupperware container to stow away terrors that, like Michael Myers, can't be killed. Only managed.

OK, here's my favorite moment in the haunted house. We're winding through the front yard of the Myers house in a foggy night sky, greenery around porch banisters, white sheets hanging out to dry. But move too fast, race too hard through the moment, and you'll miss it: Michael Myers, standing in an upstairs window, staring down at all of us, waiting.

What's the Worst Month, and Why Is It November?

Nov. 12, 2022

November is a weird one, folks. I used to think August was the worst month, but after reviewing recent data that has surfaced from a pile of Smarties wrappers on my desk, I think I could be wrong.

October is one big, avoidant costume party backed by organ music. In October, people fill car trunks with mini Snickers and park outside schools, which sounds suspicious and illegal when I type it out, but is actually encouraged societal behavior. October is silly bliss. And how do we come down? How do we make the graceful transition to a new calendar page?

Elections. My God, America kicks off the next moon orbit with elections, painful rituals that are, unfortunately, central to democracy. We start November by name-calling, arguing, unlocking our basest instincts in order to win at all costs. I could go on, but I will not focus on election results. The editors asked me not to write about elections in a plea for news variety, the way a potluck host politely says, "Um, we actually already have lots of chips."

That's fine, though, because November only gets more fraught. Have you been to a youth sporting event lately? It's like "Rocky IV" out there, and I'm talking about the parents. People are in terrible moods. They're putting on those big straw hats and starting fights with children and referees, drunk on shaky knowledge of "offsides."

Mostly, I attribute grumpiness to the end of daylight saving time. Full sun now streams through both our blackout curtains and closed eyelids, followed by the sky turning black approximately ten minutes later. This circadian disaster leads right into Veterans Day, and yes, I know Veterans Day falls on Nov. 11 for a reason. Still, I don't believe our veterans deserve a cat making muffins on their heads at 3 a.m. because Mr. Leopold Meowmers thinks it's time for breakfast.

It will take weeks, maybe months, for us to heal. But we don't have that kind of time. Because, after all this discord, we're supposed to end November thankfully? In lockstep harmony celebrating Thanksgiving? Reciting entries from gratitude journals while encircling a woefully freezer-burned unit of poultry no one actually likes? A turkey that, haha, costs 28% more than last year? We're supposed to invite the furry green guy to dinner and be all "Fah Who Foraze, Dah Who Doraze" after he called someone a... what was it... a "worn out old donkey"?

This is sounding ranty, so I want to inject some positive highlights for November. Time to consult the Old Farmer's Almanac, that compendium of wholesome trivia.

OK, Nov. 16 is National Button Day. That's promising, right? That's probably a really big deal for, you know, buttons and those who love them. According to terrible colonial folklore, November is also an ideal time to set out beaver traps and chop wood. So, we have that going for us. Beavers. Wood.

Maybe November is a quiz to pass. A challenge. Can we dig deep and be decent to each other after withstanding so many yard signs and oversized mailers? Why are the mailers so big? Can we attend T-ball without being charged with disorderly conduct? Can we donate food, check on a neighbor, offer decorative buttons to someone who might appreciate them more? Can we walk this strange bridge under the limp Macy's parade balloons, through the gentle hug of the National Dog Show, arriving intact at another seasonal playland of candy and glitter? Ask me again at 3 a.m. when my eyes pop open.

Fall Candles Are Life and Nothing Else Matters

Oct. 22, 2022

Spiced Apple Butter. That's the scent permeating my home office. Torrents of it flickering from a three-wick wax glob in a frosted jar tinted orange. One Bic burst and I'm in ... Salem? Maybe, uh, the Finger Lakes? In the glow, my incontinent senior cat becomes a kindly kitchen woman in a prairie skirt. "Come in from the cold, child," she says, churning boiled apples.

Sure, it may be a dreadful weekday, bringing with it a new credit score, but the vibes are immaculate. Spiced Apple Butter pours from the walls like in "The Shining." I'm mixing metaphors, but that happens on a psychedelic scent journey. This movie ends better. Instead of freezing to death, Jack Torrance gets his LIFE together, wrapping himself in an infinity scarf.

Because he has a candle. Anything is possible with a fall candle, the most powerful candle of all the candles. Fall is the Olfactory Olympics, and we are medalists in soft jammies. That's three metaphors in three paragraphs. Sniff. AH.

I purchased Space and Time's Spiced Apple Butter candle from JoAnn Fabrics and Crafts, a morass of autumnal senescence. Having burned through my Ashland Maple Pumpkin Butter candle from competing craft emporium Michael's, it was time for a replacement. I pondered Salted Pumpkin, which might just be a yam? Yam Candle doesn't sound enticing, I concur. Harvest Fig brought to mind the annual reverie of the family fig harvest! Spiked Cider, drunk. And Candy Corn, which ... pass.

You're asking, can all this fake sugar be healthy? Scented candles do emit chemicals, but most researchers say the risk is negligible unless you're especially sensitive or locked in a room burning a candle for days. Which, um. Moving on.

American homes have enjoyed electricity for a century, and yet, here we are, turning off the little lights and straining to read our little books next to a little fire giving off little fumes of gourd. Analysts at the NPD Group noted sales of candles, reed diffusers and home scents grew by more than 20% last year. Folks were buying more candles in 2020, too, along with self-help books and massagers. Consumers are locked in fortresses, seeking apocalyptic escape, Serenity by Jan.

Have you been to a Bath & Body Works? Bathed in the aroma of Pumpkin Pecan Waffles, of Washington's Finest Apple Macchiato? If that's not tempting, consider a candle rooted in the tradition of stoicism, a candle named Leaves.

TikTok birthed a viral candle, of course. "I don't know who needs to hear this," said user lizscham. "But Target is selling a candle that smells exactly like the air on a 65-degree day in mid-October." She speaks of my dreams.

Perhaps no one has unlocked the candle like Lakivia and Damarces Sharkey, a Tampa husband and wife team behind Treble and Flame. Lakivia, a nurse, was a Bath & Body Works candle fan. But when she got pregnant, she wanted a natural option.

She started selling soy candles on Etsy and—here's the part I'm obsessed with—pairing them with playlists designed by Damarces. Their fall candle, November, has notes of cranberry, apple, clove, chestnut and cider and pairs with music from Jaden Smith and Frank Ocean.

"My first degree was in psychology," said Lakivia. "I know that scent and sound is all tied to memory."

There's a Danish word for that, one of those delicious linguistic morsels packed with meaning, like "backpfeifengesicht," which the Germans use to describe a face begging to be slapped. Anyway, "hygge" stems from Old Norse for "hug," and it means a sensation of coziness and safety.

The quest might look like making the apartment 66 degrees and burrito-ing in a comforter. It might look like clutching a steamy mug while Enya makes breathy noises. Or it might look like lighting up a fresh Pumpkin Banana Scone from Yankee Candle and letting that baby rage until you can no longer stomach any cultivar of winter squash. Then, it's time for Tree Farm Festival and Magical Frosted Forest.

Sniff. AH.

Reasons To Be Thankful, Big and Small

Nov. 19, 2022

Gratitude is a difficult emotion to force. Plus, it's rude to make people think fast when they are trying to fit a whole yam casserole in their mouth holes. When pressed to offer thanks around a holiday table, most folks will say something generic like, "family," or "good health," when in actuality they are not *that* thankful for their family, nor do they have *that much* good health. Pass the potatoes!

The most incisive moments of gratitude tumble from the sky when you least expect. I experienced one while listening to "Aack Cast," a podcast from comedian Jamie Loftus that takes a deep dive into the boomer legacy of the comic strip "Cathy" from Cathy Guisewite. It's fun and fascinating, I recommend it.

Anyway, Loftus spotlights a panel in which Cathy rants about balancing her checkbook. The crack is that she does so by changing banks entirely. This joke hit like a ton of chocolate bricks from my car speakers in the grocery store parking lot.

Wow, am I thankful for online banking! What an era in which to do financial business! Yes, I have balanced a checkbook, and I know some of you still do. When Elon Musk buys the internet just to crash it, your gratitude will turn toward your tiny, ink-stained ledger. You will be the last one with any reliable fiscal information. But as it stands now, today, in 2022, I am grateful for freedom from recording interest earned on line 105.

Finding thanks in moments big and small is a healthy and necessary practice. It's simply too tempting to spiral into cynicism about, well, everything. Like eating Flamin' Hot Cheetos, negativity is hard to stop cronching on once you start.

So, let's do the thanks thing again this year, shall we? In fact, let's do it every year. I'll rattle off a few gratitude action items, then you take the reins and let me know your nominations. Consider this a dry run of material to bring to dinner.

I'm thankful for:

Sides. Mashed potatoes, stuffing, cornbread casserole,

even the green beans with the wiggly gray soup on top. Turkey? Eh, it's time we admitted turkey is a great thief, robbing us of precious hours we'll never get back, only to emerge from the oven bland, dry and wholly unsatisfying, awaiting a bath of salty gravy to make it passable. Do not send me your turkey recipes.

The magnificent antitrust law pop jams that will inevitably emerge from the Taylor Swift Ticketmaster debacle. And, you know, maybe enforcement of antitrust laws?

Friends with useful advice for how to make oatmeal taste less terrible.

Intrepid families who wake up to run 5Ks on Thanksgiving. Drowsy families who look at each other across the room and decide, without uttering a single word, to sleep in.

Phlebotomists who can find a spiderlike vein quickly.

A fire pit on a crisp night, tray of graham crackers, Hershey's and marshmallows at the ready.

Finding that gift you know will surprise and delight a kid who aged out of surprise and delight.

People-watching on a Sunday in the company of a perfect snarky companion.

Dogs. That's it, just dogs. Fine, cats, too.

Those helping families power through these dire economic times. Those who stepped up to help and inform Hurricane Ian survivors: the rescue workers, the journalists, the rebuilders. Those who lost so much, who have so little to be thankful for this year yet are still doing their best.

The fact that hurricane season is almost over.

The fact that election season is almost over.

All of you. Yes, all of you. Even you, over there. Yes, you. No, not her. You. You know who you are. Thank you.

Holiday Gift Exchange Rules for Misanthropes

Dec. 17, 2022

My family received a surprising number of gift exchange invites this year. I RSVP'd by lowering my spectacles and telling Bob Cratchit to fetch the coal scuttle.

At some point, I forgot how any of this works. The ongoing Triple COVID Mega Flus have mentally erased a preponderance of minor social customs. I already screwed up and told my stepkid to sign her Secret Santa gift—I thought at the event, they would... find out? Now there's a stern woman behind me ringing a bell and shouting "SHAME."

Next up, White Elephants? Yankee Swaps? Dirty Santas? Pollyanna somethings? All I know is, I bring a wrapped gift and we violently brain each other with pine-scented candles and spice blends from TJ Maxx.

This weekend looms large for parties. In all seriousness, these events serve the important function of forcing us out of our depressive bubbles and subverting the season's consumerism just a bit. Laughs! They're healthy!

I've done research to brush us all up on gift swap rules, so keep this handy as you scramble to buy a generic present for that ancillary acquaintance in your life.

SECRET SANTA

This ritual occurs in a social group such as a softball team, book club or family with 36 cousins. Although certain members may be friends, personal knowledge has no place in Secret Santa. Names are drawn at random; people are paired against their will.

Beth draws Robert, whom she has met three times. Robert has a cat, does something with "accounts" and once attended an Eagles concert. He chose "The Midnight Library" for book club, which Beth hated.

Beth now finds herself budgeting for &#%$*! Robert, in addition to family and friends. She cannot ask Robert what he might like, either, because this is SECRET. And secrets are

FESTIVE.

Beth chooses a necktie with cats on it. She writes "ROBERT" in Sharpie on a crumpled, ancient gift bag. Robert unwraps the tie and cringes. He tries to guess the giver, an impossible task because no real friend would give him this tie.

Robert and Beth share an awkward laugh. Beth refills her gluhwein and examines her lavender hand lotion set from Alicia, who joined book club last week. Robert takes the tie home to lie in wait, until he is invited to...

WHITE ELEPHANT

Each guest must bring a wrapped gift. The limit is $25, but "limit" means "spend $30 or you will look cheap." The host says, "Be creative!" which, at this point in December, feels like pliers to the toenails.

Robert wraps the cat necktie.

Everyone draws a number, determining the gifting order. Veronica gets to choose first. She scans the pile for packages shaped like liquor bottles. She opens a cat necktie. Robert eyes her apologetically.

The guests unwrap a beach cover with an image of a sexy lady body, six bottles of bad grocery store wine, a $25 Visa gift card, a Squatty Potty and a baked potato from Stan, who thinks he's funny but actually has a lot of problems.

Patricia, the party host, is three chardonnays deep and decides to spice things up. Behold...

DIRTY SANTA

Since no one is happy with their gifts, it's time to channel the spirit of the season and engage in grand theft. As everyone gets drunker, the rules get proportionally more complex.

Patricia explains that everyone can, hic, pick a new gift from the pile or steal someone else's gift. Participants may steal once per round, ensuring this game will run until the return of daylight saving time.

Veronica waits for someone to steal the cat necktie, but the room is consumed by the Squatty Potty. Even Robert, distracted by quitting the book club via text message, wants the Squatty Potty. Order gone, chaos reigns. Paper numbers litter the ground.

Patricia has somehow secured all six bottles of grocery store wine and gone to sleep.

Robert heads home with the Squatty Potty. Good for Robert, you know? Veronica leaves with the cat necktie. It will rest until next year, when an ominous holiday Evite appears from her hot yoga club. The whole ordeal starts anew, cat necktie living on ad infinitum, all powerful, forever.

Beware the 7 Types of Christmas Shoppers

Dec. 11, 2021

Christmas is three days away! Fine, it is more than three days away, but the number will register as "three" in your stress-addled brain. Compounding the dissolution of time, the supply chain is on holiday in Branson, Missouri.

Time is running out to order those special gifts loved ones will store in the back of a closet until moving to a new home (wine rack in the shape of HMS Victory). The hour is nigh to return to physical stores.

Some say in-person retail is dead, but they have not set foot in a Home Goods in December. They have not ducked behind an end cap (scented candles) to avoid someone whose line of vision is obliterated (holiday throw pillows). Stores are still substantial hubs of mayhem!

As you venture out to finish your holiday list (Bluetooth grilling thermometer), it's helpful to remember the types of shoppers you may encounter. Preparation is the greatest gift (besides a self-watering orchid pot).

STUNT DRIVING SHOPPER

Parking lots are a privilege, not a right. Does he not know this? He will Tokyo drift around the corner at Macy's while using talk-to-text and filming for TikTok. He will back his Land Rover into the moped spot. He might eject an unwilling participant from the vehicle to stand in a parking space so no one else can have it.

MANY HAPPY RETURNS SHOPPER

It's hard to believe she could not find any time except days before Christmas to seek refunds on items purchased in October (artisan cheese board, Ugg slippers). Yet here we are, waiting in line 24-deep while four clerks try to reach someone named "Joanna," the only one with the little key to do a return without a receipt.

'THIS WAS ON THE WRONG RACK' SHOPPER

Not to be confused with "I Must Inspect This (Box of Tapas Plates) And Block the Aisle" Shopper and "This (Pair of Socks) Has a Thread Hanging Down" Shopper.

NO-SHOPPING SHOPPER

She wanders Target with a list of 11 people but cannot make a decision. Is this (smoothie maker) cool or stupid? Do people still use (1,000-piece puzzles)? She clutches only the bottle of dishwashing liquid she needs for home.

PERSONAL CONVERSATION SHOPPER

They love loitering, conducting all conversations near the most popular display (chihuahua staircase). They are trying to buy a house but need to raise their credit score. Their friend is getting married to the wrong person. They cannot believe what happened on "Succession." They will tackle any subject, except, crucially, moving out of the way.

CONFUSED RELATIVE SHOPPER

Tragically, he forgot to check the ages of nieces and nephews before purchasing gifts. Those children were 6 once, yes. But they are now in college and do not want a JoJo Siwa hair bow anymore. JoJo Siwa does not even want a JoJo Siwa hair bow anymore.

ACTUALLY SHOPPING FOR MYSELF SHOPPER

Is this you? Are you strolling local boutiques under the guise of shopping for a dad (sweater that says DAD) but leaving with bags of items for yourself (nail polish kit, discount fall decorations, yet one more plant)? You're good. Just be careful with the car on the way out, lest you check two boxes.

Dating Profiles for Generic Holiday Gifts

Dec. 24, 2022

The following are five dating profiles written by last-minute holiday gifts looking for a loving partnership this season.

WHISKEY STONES

Hi! I am a set of six soapstone cubes designed to cool liquor without watering it down. I'm looking for a stable home and a drink, lol! No, literally, that's my whole thing. Anyway, I said I'd swear off online dating, but after spending four years rotating between Father's Day and Christmas endcaps at JCPenney, I'm ready to settle down. I'm seeking someone who loves whiskey, or at least lies about loving whiskey in social settings. I'd love an uncle, maybe, or a husband who spends time in the office at 2 a.m. Most weekends, I can be found hanging out on gift guides under the header "For Him," next to leather goods, gourmet hot sauce, barbecue tools, Bluetooth headphones and On Cloud sneakers. Who is "him"? No one knows, haha. I'm a package deal, in that I come with stainless-steel tongs. I hope you can accept and love them as much as I do.

SCENTED CANDLE

Hey, baby. Let me help you relax, cast a soft glow over your pile of dirty macaroni and cheese bowls, flicker softly while you scroll Get Ready With Me TikToks. You're sick of reading these disingenuous dating profiles where everyone promises adventure, aren't you? Well, that's not me. I'm not taking you on any mountain bike rides, Princess. I'm here to scent your already vanilla life with... well, um, vanilla. Specifically Warm Vanilla Sugar Cookie. I am a three-wick, glass jar girlie in a scent everyone loves because it calls to mind baking without all the work of actual baking. I am $8.99, which is within the Secret Santa budget. Take me home today and I will soften the misery of your existence, or the miserable existence of your closest work acquaintance. I don't know what to do with my bulbous lid, either.

LOTION

Three words to describe me are: emollient, emulsifier and

humectant. Yeah, I guess I'm kind of the brainy one, which is ironic because I'm so underestimated. I have a reputation as the worst last-minute gift of all the gifts. They say I convey, "I literally know nothing about you except that you have skin." But, listen, I'm really complex, and I'm looking for someone who realizes this. Like, Scented Candle is not out here increasing stratum corneum water. Ask Whiskey Stones what he knows about intercellular lipid bilayers. Oof, here I go, making this about others again. I haven't been this triggered since I got rejected from Bath & Body Works and demoted to Walmart. Lighten this up, Lotion, lighten this up. I am... let's see, what's fun about me? I'm Hibiscus Coconut. I am pink. I have shimmer. I will give your epidermis a smooth, protective layer. I deserve love, too.

LIQUOR GIFT SET

Whaaazaaaaaaaaaahhhhhhh!!?! SWIPE RIGHT!!! Grab me on your way to the White Elephant and you won't be disappointed!!!!1!! Your friend who receives me might be disappointed, because no one really wants a keepsake glass inscribed with RUMCHATA, but once they crack me open, it's on like Donkey Kong!!! I'm just a good time! I don't take life too seriously, YOLO, no FOMO! Mix me with my friend Fireball Gift Set! She comes with mini Solo cup ornaments! More the merrier, if you know what I mean!!! Get Crown Royal Gift Set and their cut glass tumblers on the horn! Paging Gentleman Jack Gift Set and his holiday sour mix!! Life of the party right here, and I come in peppermint bark flavor!! Let's puke!!

MUG

I'm a mug. My favorite book is "The Catcher in the Rye." I hate fakeness. I hate drama. I hate bad attitudes. I'm a mug. I'm looking for a 10 who cooks and doesn't have issues. I hold liquids. The front of me says "I Hate Mondays," which is funny, because everyone hates Mondays. People say I'm really funny. I like to sit in cabinets that are really full with other mugs. My handle sticks out and makes the door hard to close. I'm a mug. If you talk to me about your ex-mug, we're done. Not gonna lie, I want someone hot. I'm hot. I'm a mug.

I've Got Some Questions About Christmas Gnomes

Dec. 10, 2022

I have an urgent question: Where did all these gnomes come from?

I'm talking gift-shop gnomes, not garden gnomes. Soft and haunted. Oversized, conical Christmas hats covering everything but their bulbous noses and snowy ZZ Top beards. Bodies thick like baked potatoes. The thin, floppy lower extremities of someone who has skipped leg day for decades. Sometimes, no legs at all, just a round rump or oversized shoes protruding straight from the bum.

Why are these gnomes everywhere? Yes, I know you're going to write and say that gnomes are nothing new, that you've been collecting them for years, and where have I been on this gnome thing? It's entirely possible I'm experiencing a frequency illusion, a gnome Baader-Meinhof moment, and ever since I've started to notice the gnomes, I can't stop seeing them.

Or am I right? Have the felty, knitty variety of Christmas gnomes slowly replaced Santa Claus as the chosen mythical bon vivant of holiday decor? They perch atop all store shelves in December, not-stare-staring with their non-eye-eyes, piles upon piles of gnomes multiplying inside unsuspecting TJ Maxx and HomeGoods stores like Gremlins who have been fed past midnight. Decorative signs and whimsical sweaters abound: GNOME FOR THE HOLIDAYS. HANGING WITH MY GNOMIES. TAKE ME GNOME TONIGHT.

For the holiday influencer, Target has aesthetic gray fabric gnomes. One gnome from Pottery Barn is just a disembodied head. A set of Amazon gnome heads light up, luring innocents into their night swept clutches. Gnomes! Hugging candy canes, topping trees, sledding, standing alarmingly still, laughing their muffled, demented laughs because they have no mouths of which to speak!

I did a little research to learn about gnomes. Let me preface this by saying that Christmas traditions are bizarre all over the world. Like, let's pause and remember that Americans widely circulate a story in which a senior citizen with excess subcutaneous fat flies through the night sky on a sleigh pulled by a sassy pack of caribou, then squeezes his considerable frame down chimneys, and, I guess, jimmies apartment door locks in order to leave presents for children, but only good children. Bad children get literal coal. They get a nonrenewable energy resource. That will show them!

OK, so now that we've established that there is no good Christmas folklore, let's discuss gnomes. Christmas gnomes are Scandinavian, translated to "nisse" or "tomte." They are friendly goblins who live on farms. According to Scandification, a thorough Scandinavian guide with a winning name, gnomes originate from the souls of the farm's first owner: "Inhabitants throughout Scandinavia had to live through dark, long winters. The Scandinavian gnomes sprang from the imaginations of people who wanted to feel less alone during these cold months."

I get it! I would also hallucinate gnomes when isolated on a farm in the dead of a European winter while eating the last of the bread! Absofruitly! Much like Santa, gnomes are thought to bring presents to children, raising yet more questions of physics.

That's a lovely origin story, I suppose. It's just that Americans had to go and overdo it as usual by pumping gnomes into every possible nook of monetary gain, causing a one-person backlash (me). We also don't know when to cancel our television series.

I don't trust these gnomes, not in this quantity, not one bit. To be clear, I don't trust Santa either and don't want him in my house looking at my stuff. But I feel confident that I could take him out if he started to act sus. Like, if Santa started poking into my medicine cabinets, I could wang him behind the knees with a bottle of St. Bernardus and call for help.

Gnomes? By the dozen? Popping all around the living room at midnight with their spooky tater-tot bods and leaving beard hair on the rug? I could not defend myself against this attack. I'd be laid out, tied to a chair with evergreen branches and holly while the gnomes robbed me of all my porridge. It's simply a numbers game.

In conclusion, I've got one more jolly-sweater phrase to consider for this holiday season: JUST SAY GNOME.

(I'm so sorry.)

Petition to Cancel the Week Between Christmas and New Year's

Jan. 1, 2022

ERASE THE WEEK BETWEEN CHRISTMAS AND NEW YEAR'S

FROM: PRETTY MUCH EVERYONE

TO: A BENEVOLENT PERSON(S) WITH POWER

WE, THE UNDERSIGNED, PROPOSE THE FOLLOWING:

Dec. 26 through Jan. 2 is pointless. Really, it is so stupid. It's like putting shoes on a baby. It is past time for this chronological inefficiency to be addressed.

Those who observe Christmas are simply on their last leg come Dec. 26. They have not slept since mid-month. They have wrapped approximately 65 boxes shaped like irregular nonagons. They have listened to "All I Want for Christmas Is You" six times a day. Their children have looked into their soul and said, "Why are you tired?"

Indeed, many do not celebrate. But that does not exempt them from stressors of the season, or Mariah Carey. The streets overflow with impish drivers and shoppers. Workplaces runneth dry with vacations, operating on skeleton crews. The few reporting are forced to hold up the whole place while the lucky ones eat margarita salt and Ho Hos.

Furthermore, it's time to acknowledge that everyone is faking it this week. Nothing of substance gets done. Do not hide! We see you watching SportsCenter on your phone!

This is no longer sustainable. We need to close.

We do not propose the dates disappear from the calendar entirely, as this would only result in a premature entry into responsibility and consumption of non-starchy vegetables. The point is no one is ready to go back to anything.

We, the undersigned, suggest all activities related to society and its ongoing operations cease from Dec. 26 to Jan. 2, at the earliest. We propose this period become a national dead zone, a foggy place of ill definition, a "Purge" without the crime.

Businesses, except for essential services, will close. It will be like early pandemic quarantine, but with just the slumber party vibe and none of the staggering dread. We will not get dressed. The hours will slink together into a heavy-breathing blob. Outdoor activities such as walking in a park or sitting on a shoreline will be permitted, but not promoted.

Anyone forced to work will be paid triple-overtime-and-a-half. They will be greeted at the punch clock with a daily gift bag, like at the Academy Awards. Congratulations on your 24-karat vape pen and three-night stay at Sandals Antigua! As further consolation, they will be excused from participating in civilization the first week of January, which is only fair.

We, the undersigned, believe this tweak to the association of humankind will result in a happier and more rational populace, reducing the potential for January antics. Now, please excuse us. We have a three-hour lunch to get to.

AGREED UPON BY:

YEAH, ALL OF US.

No Diets, No Dry January, No Stress: Gentle January Is Here

Jan. 14, 2023

Welcome, fellow Type Bs, to the dark side.

We find ourselves smack in the middle of hyperactivity heaven. January is the Olympics for Type As, prime time for people who use color-coded day planners, who slot time for "relaxation" on vacation spreadsheets, who eat the same macronutrients all week, packed each Sunday in depressing Tupperware.

These people have a concerning eye glint, as if they have foraged suspect mushrooms from a marshy part of the yard. They were raring to go Jan. 2, when holiday decorations promptly went back into labeled tubs. They hung inspirational notes on office walls, as if "DISRUPTION" written on printer paper will help staff reach Q1 goals. Many of these people can be found in the halls of Congress, cackling over an evil stick of celery.

The rest of us have gazed upon rolls of jolly Santa wrapping paper teetering against a Bissell PowerSteamer for weeks whilst sliding off our couches in the manner of slime. We are dirt people, OK? Sure, we might aspire to be a spreadsheet person, but we have not so much as glanced at a clothes hanger. We have consumed nothing but chicken wings and red blends for a fortnight, and frankly, we were not ready to stop.

Time was extra dissociative this year because our school system started winter vacation really late. Holiday joy and wonder wore off eons ago, with parents and kids left staring at each other, wondering how everyone got here. The Type B children were content to chill with Cheez-Its and iPads forever. The Type A children spent the last days getting a jump on studying Mesopotamia.

Me, I'm back from two weeks off with the family. If you are ever able to indulge in a break with no plans, I recommend it. For the first week, I battled one of 54 airborne illnesses going around and consumed too much Prince Harry media between naps. The second week, I kept napping. Why stop napping? I wandered around listening to metal music from 1999 and pondered what it might be like to never turn over a new leaf, ever again.

You see, the Hyperactivity Industrial Complex tells us we must put an end to fun. The new year brings the bill we promised to pay in December when we agreed via soulless email to "circle back" and "follow up" and "tackle this in January!!"

We must now improve. We must now rekindle bonds. We must start Whole 30 and keto and intermittent fasting. We must buy elite featherweight running shoes. We must shore up savings for the upcoming financial apocalypse. We must do Dry January like monks, but not the kind of monks who make beer.

I'll pause to remind you that none of this is real. The time between the holidays and New Year's is a construct, an abstraction, a system of values. It's like money. Money only has worth because we all agree it does. Currency is a terrific scam! The January ritual is also a scam, this practice of writing a list of flaws and self-flagellating to rebalance pleasure simply because an arbitrary date has come and gone.

There's a long, similarly arbitrary year ahead, and I propose gentleness. Gentle January. Shh, not so loud. We're not demanding goals. We're letting each other ease back in. Maybe we're trying something new in February or March. Maybe not! We're not canceling naps. Maybe we're adding naps. We're not taking away spinach artichoke dip. Please, unhand the pita.

We're not taking away the legit satisfaction Type As get from order, either. That's not really the point. Gentle January is about celebrating differences and staying out of everyone's business. If you are hyper, so be it. Just remember that many of us aren't hyper. If you find fulfillment from waking up at 5 a.m. to clean baseboards, proceed. Then come to my house and do it. I need to lie down.

Be Handy

HGTV Is Lies: Tales From Pandemic Home Renovation

Nov. 13, 2021

Here's one vexing moment in the coronavirus milieu. Many of us, stuck in our homes for unnatural stretches, looked up and went: Ew. Ew! This home is Ew!

The next step was to open Realtor.com, then realize that the real estate market had turned into an H.P. Lovecraft monster that feeds on innocent children. The next step was "fixing up the place."

We decided to refinance and renovate our 1950 ranch home, which is full of "character," another way of saying "is that mold?" Over the past year, we have been lucky to repair things in desperate need, such as whole house re-piping. This is the most boring use of money. No host has ever said, "Grab your wine and I'll show you my new sink tailpiece."

After a near electrical fire and 87 deployments of the phrase "Just checking in!" with COVID-19 weary receptionists, we got to the big daddy: two pink bathrooms. I needn't explain "pink bathrooms," need I? For emphasis, I will add that one of the walls was literally falling off.

Years of renovation television prepared me. This would be a fun project! We would appear in jewel-tone sweaters, clutching our mouths. We might weep and say, "This will mean so much to (fictional family member with dramatic story of redemption)."

Many months later, we have realized hard truths:

There is no telegenic host.

Even if you've hired labor, you are on your own. Design choices, budget, learning what a "Schluter" is—you figure it out.

Each day buying grout at Floor and Decor, I prayed for a Property Brother. Just ONE Property Brother. He would show up in low-rise jeans and a too-small flannel and say things like, "Do you want the good news or the bad news? The bad news is, we've found only fettuccine Alfredo in the wall, and fettuccine Alfredo is not up to code. The good news is, I think we can offset the cost by cutting three potted plants from the Big Reveal. Why don't you head back to the hotel?"

There is no hotel.

Wisdom is life lived, or something? Our demolition preparations for the master bathroom were to push the bed out of the way and do a dance like Michigan J. Frog. That's when the contractor mentioned the word "uninhabitable."

On TV, people move out and live with mysterious benefactors. In the real world, who can just move out? In the real world, you limply drape plastic around your stuff and sleep on the couch, or on a concoction involving an ottoman and a phalanx of throw pillows. Then you jolt awake when the crew comes in and turns on Journey's greatest hits.

And there is no Big Reveal.

After shipping delays, rescheduled inspections and exploratory curse words, you'd think finishing would be electrifying. But I don't even know if I like the bathrooms anymore. Objectively, they are beautiful. But I've looked at them too much now, like staring directly into the sun.

When Chip and Joanna Gaines take someone into a room, I imagine an ecstasy of subway tile and ironic antique bicycles. Maybe after the crew leaves, homeowners hold a magnifying glass to the place where the Schluter meets the drywall and say, "Is our foundation crooked?" But it must be worth it for those minutes of bliss.

In conclusion, my home renovation advice is to get on television. Everything is better there.

I Accidentally Put My Number on HomeAdvisor and Now I Perish

Jan. 22, 2022

"A Fool's Journey," by William Shakespeare's lesser cousin, Phil Shakespeare:

The fool notices a dead tree in the yard, all black and gnarled. Branches are falling into the street, squirrels screaming. The tree must come out.

The fool knows it's time to get estimates for tree removal, one of the least fun ways to spend money outside of dental work and bail.

The fool Googles "tree removal near me."

The fool discovers a website for what seems like a small, family-owned company in her area. Even better, it has a handy little box to request an estimate. The fool loves that kind of convenience, for she is a fool!

The fool does not stop to question anything. The fool has not learned any lessons over a lifetime of lessons. Not one little lesson in her little lesson-free life.

The fool puts her contact information into the form.

The fool gets an autoreply saying sorry, the small, local company cannot do the job, but they are checking with some of their friends. Friends? Who, the fool wonders? Ross and Rachel?

The fool panics. The fool is no longer just a fool. She is a clown. She is the Joker, the Joaquin Phoenix one.

The clown immediately receives an email that reads, "Thanks for using HomeAdvisor! Here are the pros we matched to your tree removal project."

The clown did not mean to use HomeAdvisor! The clown has been tricked! The clown wanted to "do her own research," but not in the bad way!

The clown's phone immediately starts ringing, and it does not stop for the rest of the bedeviled day, filling with voicemail after voicemail from tree removal people, each hungrier to remove her twisted tree, their tongues lashing. They do not know that the true dead timber now resides within the clown's very soul.

The clown, overwhelmed, shuts down completely and doesn't answer a single call. Although these service providers will give her what she seeks, which is a quote, she is the emotional equivalent of Don Draper in season six. There's just nothing there.

The clown has one move left, which is to tweet that she is a clown. Maybe someone will see it. Maybe no one. It doesn't matter. She's a prisoner of someone named Angie, or maybe it's Angi, or maybe it's Powered By Angi; she is not sure.

The clown's tweet, against all odds, reaches a friend who also has dead trees. He sends along a phone number for the kind of tree guy who is not on HomeAdvisor. The kind of tree guy who has no website, no online forms, who may be best reached by flare gun, actually. The kind of tree guy who is not expecting her call, but has a chainsaw, and is willing to use it.

The clown sheds a tear. She will call. First, she gazes once more upon the ashen, twisted limbs. The phone chimes again, and again, and again.

Real or Fake? Listings for Half-Million Dollar Homes

June 18, 2022

As the country's distended housing market evolves like a deranged Pokemon, you may have been tempted to peruse a local open house. Or, you may have developed a habit of neurotically browsing real estate listings, wondering how long you will be captive in your current situation. Haha, who would do that???

As the Federal Reserve plans to tamp down the economy and reset the out-of-control home market, house sales are finally cooling off. The bonkers real estate listings, though, will not be stopped so easily. They embody *le spirit of the times* : "With a little ingenuity, a fifth loan and a yearslong commitment to cohabitating with a contractor named Timmy, you might be able to get, eh, 20% closer to the home of your dreams. Room for pool!"

To pass time until the inevitable financial fallout, let's play a game. The following listings are from the Tampa Bay region of Florida, site of one of the largest home price spikes in the nation. Your mission is to decide if these spots for homes in the $500,000 range are real, or if I made them up. The answer key is at the bottom. Don't cheat, unless unimportant acts of rebellion make you feel alive in a world evading your understanding, in which case, proceed.

No. 1: Opportunities abound for the creative buyer. Kitchen pantry could be converted into a home office, nursery, wet bar or reading nook.

No. 2: Paint throughout!

No. 3: 5 min to the new TESLA FACILITY.

No. 4: Sip coffee while gazing on a retention pond water view from three exposures.

No. 5: This is not in a flood zone like most homes in the area.

No. 6: Location, location, location! Only six miles from Publix, 12 miles from middle/high school and a quick 45-minute drive to restaurants, shops and nightlife.

No. 7: You could rehab this cozy home and sit poolside, you could tear it down and build your dream home in one of South Tampa's most desirable neighborhoods, or you could build a second home on the property and use it as an in-law suite or a rental opportunity (buyers are encouraged to do their due diligence and confirm with City and County exactly what is allowed).

No. 8: Historic smell will transport you to another era.

No. 9: Let's start with the front porch. In a time before the hustle and bustle that we live in now there were front porches. A place to congregate with neighbors and sip on your favorite beverage, a nice opportunity to unwind before dinner.

No. 10: Situated just steps from the highway, the sound of cars will lull you to sleep at night. Easy airport access!

No. 11: Has a tenant you can keep if you wish, he has no lease, month to month.

No. 12: Sold as is. Needs extensive renovation, priced accordingly.

No. 13: The Family Room could be a 3rd Bedroom. There is a Large Closet That Allows for A Lot of Storage Space. The Current Owner used it as an Additional Pantry, Storage, And for Hanging Clothes. The Washer/Dryer in the Garage used to be in the Closet in the Family Room... plumbing is still there so very easy to move back.

No. 14: All windows fully functional, roof in place, floors level, termites have been recently eradicated.

No. 15: Open the slider doors and windows during the cool months and your guests can move about with ease.

No. 16: This home boasts a kitchen.

No. 17: And when you have yard waste, no worries, there is an abundance of receptacles.

No. 18: Washer & dryer doesn't convey!

No. 19: Neighbor with large political flags bearing F-word is actually nice guy.

No. 20: This Saint Petersburg one-story home offers a patio.

Key: 1) fake; 2) fake; 3) real; 4) fake; 5) real; 6) fake; 7) real; 8) fake; 9) real; 10) fake; 11) real; 12) real; 13) real; 14) fake; 15) real; 16) fake; 17) real; 18) real; 19) fake; 20) real.

This Toilet Can Flush Golf Balls, and I Have Existential Dread

May 1, 2021

I found it. The moment technological advances became so powerful they were rendered irreversible. The fulcrum of a changed human experience.

A toilet that can flush golf balls.

Inside a Lowe's, the world folded in on itself like a neutron star grown too large. Was I imagining this? The box in the toilet aisle read:

ENGINEERED TO PREVENT CLOGS

FLUSHES A BUCKET OF GOLF BALLS IN A SINGLE FLUSH

Therapists say you should sit in your discomfort. My husband, sensing I needed time, shuffled off to look at cabinet pulls.

It was the American Standard Champion 4, which sounds like a heroic golden retriever. This collection was introduced years ago, an exciting addition to the world of powerful plumbing. I have never claimed to be a breaking news reporter. They are popular in both homes and hotels, motto: "We are tired of coming to the room at 2 a.m. to see about a clog."

This commode haunted me. We are in the middle of double bathroom renovations, and each decision feels like the most important and least important thing in the world. I have projected all anxieties about troublesome global events onto the EXACT. RIGHT. TILE. Have you ever heard the word "Schluter"? You have now. It's as relaxing as watching "Uncut Gems."

Could the perfect toilet really exist, flushing all ills? If mankind can create an ADA-compliant, comfort-height throne with a large trapway that flushes with the power of the Titan gods of the four winds, does that mean there is hope for this broken world?

We are perpetually lectured by bathroom stall notes. Usually, it's a straightforward request to flush only toilet paper. Or it's a whimsical rhyme, like: "What's this poem all about? Flush your tissue and get out!" Then, worst of all—there's the passive-aggressive missive, written by the same anon who posts that the office microwave "doesn't clean itself."

With good reason, though! There is something called a fatberg, which is a disgusting sewer blockage of all the bad things people flush. And American Standard doesn't want us to flush weird things, either, of course. Golf balls are a marketing stand-in for, um, you know.

But it can flush golf balls, and there is Toilet Content online to prove it. Have you ever spent a Monday morning watching toilet vids on company time? Don't answer that. There's one of a kid throwing in Barbie heads, miniature bottles of Pert Plus, stuffed animals and bras. You can watch flushing marshmallows, banana peels, cat litter, hot dogs, rubber tubes and miso paste.

If you'd like to further exacerbate your break from reality, delve into the world of super high-end toilets, like the one made of solid gold in Hong Kong or the one covered in Swarovski crystals in Japan. Briefly, it will make you forget about any looming constitutional crises.

And yet, nothing is perfect, not even the seductive golf ball latrine. You will know this, because your next stop will be toilet review websites. We are always flushing forward in pursuit of something better.

Then, I learned about American Standard's "VorMax Flush Technology: The Cleanest Flush Ever Engineered," and time froze across a primordial black hole.

Cleaning Up So Contractors Like Me

July 15, 2023

Tell me why I loaded the dishwasher before "Brian" came over.

Tell me why I cannot welcome any contractor from any home repair company to simply analyze drywall cracks, inspect the foundation and offer one of three estimates without worrying about how the stupid little interior of the house looks, the least of my problems.

Tell me why I am compulsively convinced my home is the messiest, most disastrous abode a construction professional has ever set foot inside, the same way I am convinced my body is the most repulsive one the dermatologist has ever encountered during the annual skin cancer screening. Tell me why I assume all the other homes workers visit look like the luxe New Jersey manor of Carmela Soprano that time she changed out her bathroom wallpaper.

Tell me why I put away the party-sized bottle of Absolut vodka right before Brian's arrival, hiding the moat of clear liquor that was only out in the open because we recently had a party that necessitated a party-sized bottle of vodka. Tell me why I didn't want Brian thinking I was sitting around drinking from a party-sized bottle of vodka at 9:55 a.m. Tell me why I need Brian's moral endorsement.

Tell me what in the trash suddenly smells so bad!!!!!

Tell me why I said, "Oh, sorry about these piles of laundry!" as if he randomly caught me doing a cute chore, when the truth is that the piles of laundry are always there, shape-shifting into a novel Lusus Naturae of pants and T-shirts and socks and bras.

Tell me why it is so terrible to be perceived.

Tell me why I am convinced Brian will be nice to my face but later convene with other home improvement specialists at the pub and talk about this one lady who had a troubling number of costume wigs and realistic foam Renaissance weapons.

Tell me why I just asked Alexa to play lo-fi hip-hop in the

background.

Tell me why I care if a person I've asked to crawl beneath my house in the mud and mold and rat droppings, someone I may never see again in all my natural days, someone who is likely not going to insult me because he would like to sell me goods and services, glimpses the nonstick pan in which I recently made grilled cheese. Tell me what difference it will make if Brian sees a tumbleweed of cat hair beneath the TV console, or a pile of credit card offers on the table, or a rumpled Hello Kitty sleeping bag last used in a living room pillow fort. Tell me how my home's current structural problems will disappear if, during this 90-minute business consultation, Brian finds himself transported to a more pleasant mental space, as if he is having a steam facial at the Waldorf Astoria and not explaining various methods of steel jacking and mold entrapment.

Tell me why I lit a candle.

Be Messy

Look at my Tiny Dog if You Feel Dead Inside

Jan. 18, 2021

I regret to inform you that this is a dog column. I know. I am sorry, but this is how it has to be.

You see, there is a secret society for columnists who write about the "lighter side of life." We meet in a warehouse and take an oath; it involves a Zippo, an ace of spades and a banana peel. We are assigned a catchphrase like, "Get a load of this!" We are told to find a wacky, endearing dog to be a character in the column.

Problematic. When I was an editor and commuting, we kept our menagerie limited to the cat, Countess. Her activity level is set at "ricotta cheese." This job is more flexible. And in quarantine, we suddenly had enough time on our hands to pave a highway.

Husband requested we get what scientists call a "brown dog," something that came out of a laundry basket in an alley. Boxhead would ride in a bicycle sidecar and stand on the end of kayaks. Rough, tumble, sturdy, noble, athletic.

So he should have paid more attention when I flashed him the animal rescue Facebook page on a Friday between virtual meetings. If he didn't drop everything to notice I was showing him an extremely tiny purebred Pomeranian that needed a foster home, well, I can't help him.

"How is he with cats?" Josh murmured, which loosely translates to, "I am noncommittal about this whole thing."

Reader! If you see a rescue animal of interest on social media, follow instructions. More than 600 people commented on the photo of this dog, including me ("How is he with cats?"). But apparently, I was first to use the requested email. What felt like minutes later, staff asked if we could come to the Palm Harbor shelter today.

We had never fostered a dog. I had a dog once who I loved deeply. Stuart died six years ago, and I didn't have any of his stuff anymore. We were not ready for this. But what else were we going to do with an endless order to stay home? Parcheesi?

He was 4 years old, 5 pounds, matted, had fleas and needed to be neutered. He was hunched and crept around like a Stygian witch.

Josh is 6-foot-2 and used to be an offensive lineman. He held the warm ball of soot and disintegrated. Time to go home!

The dog came with the name Gizmo, like in "Gremlins." But the first time he stood up and made voracious love to a dog bed, I knew he looked more like Rocket Raccoon from "Guardians of the Galaxy."

Look, you know this ends with us keeping him. How could we not? The finale of this column will not be the cake we made him upon adoption, the horrible, unspeakable cake that looked like a cow patty.

The surprise twist is the one in our crusty hearts. This furry piece of coal refocused our compassion for animals, yes, but also people.

We don't know who had him before, and at first, we judged a bit. But when we went back to adopt, a volunteer recognized the raven Tribble. An old man had dropped him off, she said, struggling to get to the door. His wife was ill, and they had to move in with someone. They couldn't take the dog.

The good people at animal shelters are carrying on through this pandemic, and thankfully, more people are interested in fostering and adopting. Amid untold economic and personal turmoil, most of us are doing what we can.

I believe this pooch's people loved him and were doing what they could. It must have been very hard to let him go with a question mark.

So, whoever you are, here's the deal. We call him Rocket. There's an 8-year-old who is his soul mate. They play and run and cuddle. He still makes that gurgling noise like a small dinosaur. He eats out of a soy sauce dish, one piece at a time. He plays with hair ties. He had surgery and no longer accosts pillows. He is on joint supplements. He has gained one-tenth of one pound, and his magnificent Pomeranian ruff is coming in.

We're happy with him. And we think he's happy with us.

Shortly after I finished writing this, he peed on the rug.

I Am Powerless Around a 50/50 Raffle and Apologize for Nothing

Oct. 30, 2021

Tom Brady is not returning my calls, but I've heard from other sources that we're in the thick of sports season. That means it's time to “tackle” (ha-ha) a topic oft-debated by the global intelligentsia:

50/50 raffles.

A 50/50 raffle is lovely in its simplicity. Folks put money into a pot, and the winner splits the final take with a charity. The more people who buy in, the bigger the payday.

Fun fact: 50/50 raffles might be illegal where you live. In many states, an organization cannot require payment to enter, only suggest a donation. I am sorry if that causes infighting at this winter's Historic Homes Wine-Around, when Trevor insists he does not have to pay by law.

Big sports teams have their patooties covered with legal disclaimers, of course, and no one really enforces raffles at the wing-joint cancer fundraiser. Maybe that's because the enforcers are busy digging in wallets for their last $20.

Or is it just me? I am powerless around a 50/50 raffle, like a dog near a trash can of pulled pork.

I'm not a gambler by nature. In Vegas, I'm more likely to spend on commemorative Celine Dion merchandise than a slot machine. Lottery? Nah. “My Lottery Dream Home” usually ends with a center-unit townhouse in Racine, Wisconsin, which doesn't seem worth the trouble.

Why, then, is a 50/50 different? The charity element is key, of course. It feels better to risk cash when you know it's going to a good cause. But it's more than masking compulsion with virtue. I have thought about this a lot, typically during the final 40 minutes of a sporting event when they stop serving beer.

What we're paying for is the chance to fantasize through, oh, at least half of a game that may sometimes be, I'm sorry, boring. After spending $40 on a soft pretzel, it feels good to marinate in a daydream of becoming the Stanley Cup champion of raffles.

The sensation travels beyond sports. We visited a church fall festival, an event full of gambling and alcohol sales to raise money for the Lord's work. After having my tires rotated by a ride called Zero Gravity, I sought solace at the 50/50 table. My stepkid wondered why I would spend money on something I'm not likely to win.

"Steph doesn't really do anything bad," her father explained, because covering for my faults is his main task. "Just let her have this."

Yes, an important life lesson! Just leave your bug-eyed, craven family member alone to wallow in her toothless vice! Talk about her to your friends, if you must, but walk on!

It goes without saying that I have never won a 50/50 raffle and don't expect to. If you play, you know that, right? The odds are just incredibly bad, especially in an arena filled with 20,000 loose-wallet revelers on a third White Claw.

But you know what's priceless? Sitting through the seventh inning of a baseball game, when someone has been trying to steal third for a full 20 minutes, watching that number tick up on the big screen. Imagine how it would feel to *replace a fence* and *pay off a Visa* and *purchase a California Closets system?*

In that moment, ever brief, there is true joy.

A Last-Minute Tax Day Guide for Professional Procrastinators

April 9, 2022

Progresstination.

I accidentally uttered this recently while trying to say "procrastination." It was a Freudian slip, less a regressive childhood parapraxis and more a trauma related to the Internal Revenue Service, as one has. However, this slip revealed an abiding truth.

See, paying taxes puts the FUN in functional society, and I've never missed a deadline. That does not mean, under any circumstances, I've ever filed early. On time and early are totally different things.

Does this sound like you? Come, kin, rally around.

Tax Day is April 18 this year, three days late due to Emancipation Day in the District of Columbia. Last year, the pandemic drew out Tax Day to May 17, which was like Christmas for procrastin... progresstinators.

"Wouldn't you rather get it out of the way?" a responsible, punctual person might ask. "Get your return early? Have more time to pay? Move on, heal?"

Definitely not. To quote tax collector Friedrich Nietzsche, "Is life not a thousand times too short for us to bore ourselves?" No one is guaranteed tomorrow. If I don't make it, that's not great, but it also means I will have gotten out of doing taxes. Whose strategy sounds better now?

Progresstination, though, is pointless progress. It's a way to feel like a productive member of civilization, completing little tasks adjacent to taxes without actually doing taxes. Apply this philosophy liberally to cleaning bathrooms, renewing government identifications and having difficult personal discussions that include I-statements such as, "When you do __, it makes me feel __."

For example:

Identify tax documents in the kitchen stack of mail sorted

as "important." That stack has slumped into the pile that's "unimportant, but probably good to shred because of identity theft." That has in turn slumped into "unimportant, can go in recycling bin"—a bin, which, unbelievably, is just steps away from this pile, and yet. This special pile includes catalogs for Viking River Cruises and expensive puffer vests one might wear in a canoe.

There. Having secured all vital tax forms, move them somewhere more official such as an end table, a decorative chair or one of 40 empty filing folders you bought at Office Depot when you decided to get organized in 2012. That was a cute day.

Visit the website for your preferred tax software. Test your username, PIN number and password. It has 17 letters, four non-consecutive numbers and a special character (excluding question marks, too on the nose). Failing log-in, close the window. To quote IRS commissioner Don Draper, "Think about it. Deeply. Then forget it."

Read several articles titled "What to know for Tax Day" and initiate panic over capital gains, dividends, interest, home office expenses, 1099 forms and alleged letters regarding advance child tax credits and stimulus payments. Go back to the mail pile, which somehow now contains a new catalog of stylish polyester pants for women of a certain age.

Take a break for snacks!

Lastly, set intentions. Identify a time you WILL do your taxes. Set up a reward for yourself, other than the intrinsic one that comes with doing a civic duty at the last possible second. State it boldly: "I intend to do my taxes after the Target run, but before eating an entire pint of Chubby Hubby."

I am so proud of you.

Do You Return Your Shopping Cart, or Do You Choose Chaos?

July 16, 2022

A fruitful exercise is to ask readers what irritates them, which I do often in my newsletter. This opens a floodgate of material, from "Forms: Why does my child's swim school need the name of my dentist?" to "Golf: Ew."

This week, I heard from Cameron Spears of Odessa, Florida. He suggested I write about shopping carts, or people who don't return them. "It fascinates and annoys me," he said. Well, Cameron, same. This infraction has been chilling on my peeve list for some time.

In my wild and brazen younger years, the days of Candie's tracksuits and platform flip-flops, I admit to having dropped carts wherever. I half-credit an ex with changing my mind. Half-credit because his reasoning was, "Imagine what the cart guy could do if he wasn't busy cleaning up your carts!"

Now, returning a cart doesn't mean a store employee will peel off his name tag and become a full-time infectious disease specialist. Retail workers are plenty busy without cart negligence, and they deserve respect for what they do. But it got me thinking: I had no excuse to be a lazy sack of pink terry cloth. Putting my cart back was an easy place to start.

That relative ease is at the core of the Shopping Cart Theory, a viral meme that posits: "The shopping cart is the ultimate litmus test for whether a person is capable of self-governing. To return the shopping cart is an easy, convenient task and one which we all recognize as the correct, appropriate thing to do."

Because punishment is mostly nonexistent, the theory goes, returning a cart is intrinsic good faith. Generally, I agree this is one small thing mankind can do when we're not slapping each other to death against a backdrop of staggering galactic insignificance. But there are caveats, opportunities to press the brakes on judgment.

Scientific American went deep on cart behavior in 2017, using terms like "injunctive norms" and "descriptive norms." Anthropologist Krystal D'Costa outlined who may not comply. This includes parents who can't leave babies alone. Shoppers may have physical limitations, visible and invisible disabilities.

Then there's a more baffling cohort of rebels who believe they benevolently keep people employed by turning the Target lot into a Tough Mudder. This, friends, is mental gymnastics, and I wish you well in the Olympics!

In the name of anthropology (stalking), I spent a few hours observing (staring like a creep at) people to gauge cart compliance. I sat in my car, peering over sunglasses and sipping a large Sprite Zero with nugget ice, a discount detective. A Tampa Walmart appeared most chaotic, in contrast to the tidy Publix two miles south. By the time I got to an outdoor mall 20 miles away, buggies were in full lawless disarray: Target carts flipped over behind the building, Costco carts big enough to transport several capybaras found clear across the premises, a PetSmart cart crying out existentially.

Among the varieties of cart disposal:

Curb cart: This one is a head-scratcher. The shopper had to maneuver it off the ground into the mulch. The Apple Watch is lit after this; one wonders if a simple jaunt to the cart bay would have burned fewer calories.

Parking space cart: The worst cart! One thousand negative bonus points if the cart is in the accessible space. For shame.

Cart pushed just out of reach of shopper's car into someone else's car: Two thousand negative bonus points!

Cart right next to the cart bay: They made it all the way to the cart receptacle and then, I guess, were raptured.

Lost Boys carts: Abandoned carts that have formed a club.

Cart with mysterious open food/feasting birds: Why is it always a rotisserie chicken?

Cart moment of truth: This cart is at a crucial juncture. The shopper has unloaded three pallets of Kirkland water, a value pack of brownie bites, two electric toothbrushes and incredible quantities of pinot grigio. Shopper looks askance. Will he leave the cart? Will he walk 25 feet? Suddenly, he is saved when a woman emerges from her car in search of a cart, thus completing the cycle into...

The handoff cart: This mayhem starts all over again.

Money-Saving Gas Price Tips for Your Emotional Breakdown

March 12, 2022

Welcome, drivers. Have you noticed it costs approximately one IKEA dresser to fill a car with gas? Have you stood at the pump, gaping at the number as if witnessing a rhinoceros birth? Have you read several wonky deep dives on oil price determinants and wished you'd spent less time in economics class imagining fancy lady heads in the gum stuck to seats?

These are the tips for you!

Gas prices have climbed higher than ever, surpassing a 2008 record, with national averages well over $4 a gallon. Between the war in Ukraine, an American ban on Russian oil, supply, demand and antsy traders, prices are expected to keep going up, the way we are expected to keep waking up, incredibly. AAA, helping people avoid learning to change a tire for more than a century, has blanketed the media with fuel-saving tips. Let's examine them.

"Maintain your vehicle to optimize fuel economy."

Take the car in for a tune-up. Get an oil change, rotate the tires and... replace... wait, what filter now? For how much? OK, yeah, I guess that sounds important. Power steering pump? No, it wasn't making noise, but now that you mention it... And which fluid is dirty, exactly? What is a pulley? No, I know what a "pulley" is, but I mean... No, I had not noticed that windshield chip. I am so glad I'm saving money on gas.

"Remove excess weight in your vehicle."

Empty your trunk to lighten the load. In fact, empty your personal baggage, which is weighing down the car and your soul. Studies show people use 10% more energy when clinging to memories of a fight about "emotional unavailability" eight years ago outside a TGI Friday's.

"Enroll in savings programs."

AAA suggests a Shell program because they have a partnership. Also consider joining a bulk membership club like

Costco or BJ's for discount gas. It's fun to sit in eternal lines at the pump and block the store driveway. Lots of friendly waves with the longest finger! While you're at the store, stock up on water, nonperishable foods, headlamps, gauze, multitools, duct tape, cords to snare wild game and crowbars.

"Drive conservatively."

Ease up on the accelerator. Driving slow also provides a chance for a mental stemwinder. Start with the harrowing situation in Ukraine, then shift to internalized guilt over your relative privilege, then wonder if you're becoming that meme of a lady sitting in a comfortable house complaining about living through historic events, then decide to humbly endure gas prices to stick it to Russia, then remember a lot of people can't really afford to do that and that the working class always gets... sticken... to, which reminds you how so many state legislatures are now "The Hunger Games" Capitol of Panem with legislators guffawing over plates of fine jellies and inventing hateful nonsense laws, then cough a couple times and wonder if you have COVID-19, then recall a link a friend sent about a Japanese volcanic rock that contained a death demon until the ROCK BROKE OPEN, which really explains a lot, and then, for no reason at all, think of a dinner party the other night and how it should have been obvious you said NICE BOOTS and not BOOBS, then feel the entire surface of your skin crawl, and that brings you back to the fight at the TGI Friday's and how you weren't *wrong* about emotional unavailability, he just wasn't *listening,* which proves your *point,* then remember you are supposed to unload emotional baggage in order to save gas money, then stop because—wait—the gas light is on.

To My Laundry Chair: I Couldn't Have Done It Without You

July 17, 2021

For years, we had a lovely furniture showpiece in the bedroom. The microfiber chair from Crate and Barrel was royal blue, plush, with matching throw pillows. And for years, we did not set eyes on this chair, let alone sit in it.

Why? You know why. It was the Laundry Chair. Maybe you pretend not to have one. Perhaps you shove the laundry into a closet moments before company arrives, and then show off your elegant sitting area like it's a Victorian fainting room for recovering from boned corsets.

But you know the grisly truth. Other versions of Laundry Chair include Laundry Window Seat; Laundry Ottoman; Laundry Secretary Desk; Laundry Treadmill/Peloton; and Laundry Basket So Full It Has Become A Flat Surface For More Laundry.

Laundry Chair blends into the scenery, melting into an amorphous blob between the wall and the floor. Once the room absorbs the soul of Laundry Chair, like a haunted Ikea, Laundry Chair becomes immutable. Occasionally, it catches your eye. You think, "If I get murdered and the crime scene photos end up on '48 Hours Investigates,' this laundry situation is going to be so embarrassing."

Our showdown with Laundry Chair came suddenly. We got a new bedroom set and decided to reconfigure the space. After moving everything, the room still felt cramped and chaotic. The conversation between my husband and I went something like:

"I feel like there should be more room in here."

I eye Laundry Chair.

"Yeah, weird."

He eyes Laundry Chair.

"Maybe ... we should ..."

"Later."

Plenty of articles and blogs are devoted to "accent chairs," a phrase like "jumbo shrimp." Apartment Therapy argues that "accent chairs give you another place to play with color, pattern, and texture, but they're also a perfect spot for reading, laying out your clothes, and setting down a bag or another oft-used object."

See? Most of the paragraph is devoted to setting things on the chair.

It's time to stop the lies. There is no point in a bedroom chair. What, are you going to just ... sit? Think about international conflicts? Bedrooms are for lying flat, ruminating on failed dreams. Bedrooms are for checking your phone, even though it's harming your circadian rhythms. Bedrooms are for trying on six outfits before choosing the same black shirt and jeans you wear every day, and then placing the six outfits on Laundry Chair.

After we moved the bed, I flopped down to begin my God-ordained purpose of looking at my phone. Suddenly, laundry was flying about, and the chair was on the move.

"We need to do this now, or we'll never do it," he said. He was right.

Laundry Chair is in the living room now, where we actually sit on it. The bedroom feels much more spacious, liberated from fraudulent seating. And yet, there is a new problem. We have to put the laundry away.

In related news, I'd like you to meet my new friend: Laundry Stool.

Blahs and Bad Dreams in the Pandemic's Fourth Year

March 4, 2023

For as long as my mushy cerebral cortex has had folds, I've been blessed (or cursed) with vivid dreams. In them, my subconscious tends to take on actions I avoid in real life. For instance, I am a pretty low-conflict person. I don't enjoy fighting, and I can't remember the last time I yelled at another human. I am more likely to bottle feelings, go to bed and chew through my mouthguard during somnolent screaming matches, Academy Award-winning, guttural performances. I wake up ready to be even-keeled and likable again.

I often remember these dreams. I've read about why this happens for some people and not others, and the reasons are vast and varied. Most researchers agree, though, that we remember dreams that are so intense they shoot us awake from the depths of REM slumber. We remember the ones that really rock us.

To wit, my dream last week:

I hosted a get-together to test out my fledgling manicure and pedicure skills on close friends, skills I do not have in real life. But in this dream, I wanted to learn something new and take a low-pressure step toward becoming a nail superstar. My brain had assembled an all-star cast from the spectrum of my life: friends from middle school, high school and beyond, plus a wildly strange collection of co-workers. My co-workers are reading this wondering if I did their pedicure in a dream, but I might take that information to my grave.

Quickly, the group ballooned to 20 angry, impatient people. I realized doing manicures and pedicures on everyone would be a 24-hour affair and I was just one person. Everyone wanted something specific, complaining about the temperature of the water, demanding nail art for which I was not qualified! After finishing nails on two so-called friends and accepting that it was impossible to please everyone, I woke up from the depths of REM with a dream I have chewed on ever since.

I'm extra reflective this time of year. Early March has been riddled with outsized anxiety since 2020. Each time a social media memory pops in from moments before the pandemic's true scope emerged, it feels like a ghost of a past life floating over the bed. I recognize that person going to a party and running a 5K, but I can never fully be her again.

She isn't traumatized in the classical sense, because others endured far more loss and pain, but she has hairline fractures. She doesn't look the same, dress the same, feel the same zest about making plans. She is older and more tired, which was going to happen no matter what. But she wonders if another version of her would have popped out more spry, less tentative, with better-fitting pants.

Is this new person stuck, succumbed to the comfortable habits of home? Can she try anything new and stick with it? Can she locate her former trust in humanity, or did humanity eat it up? She wonders if the people gathered in her house for pedicures truly believe in her or if they are heavy with judgment, whispering about her inertia while staring ahead with their own dead eyes.

I can't articulate the confusing Ides of March better than Jon Mooallem in the latest New York Times magazine. He attempts to make sense of the nuance of a cultural narrative still forming. Read the entire thing, even though he acknowledges you don't want to. That is the point: "As we enter a fourth pandemic year, each of us is consciously or subconsciously working through potentially irreconcilable stories about what we lived through—or else, strenuously avoiding that dissonance, insisting there's no work to be done."

He asks, what is normal? Perhaps it's an impenetrable concept worth abandoning altogether. "The weirdness we've felt since—what's still making us wobbly now—may be the strain of trying, as hard as we can, to crank that busted machinery of normal back on," he writes.

While this one, stupid dream means I am overdue for nail services, I guess it also means whatever I want it to mean. So, I think it means this:

Blah.

We can't pretend we should be the same as the people in those pre-pandemic photos. We can't pretend to have infinite energy to please everyone we have ever known, pretend we are not cynical, bruised, harder, older, sadder. We can't pretend to be normal because normal is a construct, and constructs are handles we cling to in search of certainty.

The blah. The blah is the work. The blah is the good space, the space where we can reset, find a new goal, energy, faith, the next steps forward in this house of mirrors. Because by pushing every blah feeling down, we leave our subconscious to do the hard work in the middle of the night. It's not fair to ask the brain's default network to locate the exact right shade of blue sparkle polish for a friend who is out there walking through the same hazy, unbelievable dream.

Writer's Block Tried to Ruin Me

May 21, 2022

Acute panic accompanies a blank page, so I almost never use one. It's a mental trick. You see, I write columns in one contiguous Google document of half-shaped paragraphs and ideas, a grotesque prose jabberwocky that eventually grows too bloated to function.

My previous document got to 629 pages and 127,000 words before it froze. My current file is a third of that in various states of undress, a busker's tip jar. Throw a couple (40,000) words in, and you can fool even yourself.

Not this week. Not right now. Can you tell I have writer's block? This doesn't normally happen. I've built a catalog being fast, productive and free from the prison of overthinking. Confident writing is a muscle that develops with use, each collection of words a bicep curl. I write two columns and one email newsletter each week, and in my free time, fiction. I'm *constantly* writing. Results vary, but the words plop out and I move on.

This blockage, though, this intellectual fatberg wedged into the pipes of my right hemisphere and would not budge. In a hysterical state, I made repetitive trips to the coffee pot and sent a check-in to my editor that read, "Trying to avoid a full mental spiral, that's the update." For four days, I couldn't focus or even compose a tweet. That's 280 characters. Emojis are an option. "Real Housewives" GIFs. Photos of sloths.

There have been moments lately the internet seems so bad, so fast, so furious that no path feels distillable, entertaining or insightful. I started and stopped pieces, dashed off notes about local and world events, toyed with potential headlines, mined my drab, puny personal life.

The Google doc became a notebook found beneath floorboards of a remote cabin.

Do not waste food. Use all food in fridge! Be inspired by French.

Start a community garden? Explore logistics.
Gas is for millionaires?
Men online. Is this the end of men?

Ostensibly, "things" aren't worse today than they were yesterday, or two years ago. "Things" are bad on an ever-sliding scale. "Things" are fine for me, personally. So what? What is happening when the flow congeals?

Storied writers have issued opinions on the B-word ranging from "death is the only escape" to "it's fake." The ones who say writer's block is a myth probably don't have three standing deadlines a week.

British writer Alexander McCall Smith once told The Daily Mail that "writer's block is a load of nonsense," that he finds going to Botswana helpful to open his mind. OK, well! Then again, there was Ray Bradbury in The Paris Review with more practical advice: "I have three rules to live by. One, get your work done. If that doesn't work, shut up and drink your gin. And when all else fails, run like hell!"

It's not just writers who get stifled, right? Interior designers must have days when everything looks gray and flat. Chefs have nights when every sauce is 70% emulsified garbage. Accountants have moments when the numbers are utter nonsense. The lights flicker in every mind.

I'm tempted to blame the barrage of online stimuli, trending topics, cycles of hot takes, hot reactions to hot takes and corrections to hot reactions to hot takes. How does anyone find time to interrogate the dusty corners of the soul when there's always something shiny to see? I, for one, need to review every dress from Cannes.

My go-to remedy for writer's block is getting out of the office. Not Botswana, but, like, a coffee shop. And, of course, reading. I reached for a book this week by Mary Schmich, retired columnist from The Chicago Tribune. Let's visit page 44 of "Even the Terrible Things Seem Beautiful to Me Now":

"In moments when I have nothing with which to fill this column—which, really, is not happening right now—I recite that sentence to myself several times. Panic is my muse. Panic is my muse. Panic is my muse."

She wrote that in 1999. The internet may be rotting our brains, but panic is timeless!

In the end, relenting worked. Admitting that I was, as they say in Paris, "le losing it," shook free ideas, shook free these words. The muscle was there, hiding under a dopamine afghan, tucked inside cortical folds of doom. It just needed a nap before pressing on.

I Alone Know the Correct Temperature on the Thermostat

June 3, 2023

Relationship wisdom develops gradually, blooming as the astringent tannins of life soften. Say, for example, both parties have previously loved, lost and been through enough professional counseling to sedate a wild boar. Now older and wiser, they have settled into the kind of second-time-around partnership in which no hurdle seems that high.

They just don't *sweat*—remember that word—too much. They use "I feel" statements and cognitive mirroring techniques. They compromise. They think before speaking and follow up when *cooler*—remember it—heads prevail.

What mature partners do not do is hiss, "DON'T BE LIKE THAT" with all the warmth of a wicked forest crone. "DON'T BE LIKE THAT" is a wholly unhelpful phrase to lob at ... well, anyone. Like what? Don't be like what? Specificity is key!

And yet, 'twas I who yowled "DON'T BE LIKE THAT," because the issue at hand was the thermostat. On this topic, I struggle to access maturity. There I was, in May, in Tampa Bay, wearing sweatpants one might wear in a Vermont December, boldly clicking down the temperature in our creaky, old Florida house as my husband eyed me precariously from across the room.

"DON'T BE LIKE THAT."

Now, listen. We humans can disagree on plenty. Many issues have nuance, space for debate and concession. One might argue we all could use a half-cup more understanding to be kinder citizens of the world.

But the thermostat is not one of those issues, and I know you will agree. The right way to load a dishwasher is another, as is the direction of the toilet paper roll. These are deeply held personal convictions. There is a correct temperature, especially this time of year where I live in Florida, when tolerable mornings give way to afternoons that feel like a steaming bowl of celebrity bone broth.

I like it cold. I may be an outlier among the stereotypically cold female species, portrayed on television asking for cardigans and scolding perspiring office oafs. I am overheated most of the time, and you will find me knocking off digits as often as the law allows. I also happen to like white noise, which is an incredibly toxic trait when the air handler kicks on. Cold! Whirring! Perfect!

Moreover, I like it *cozy.* In order to be cozy, I need to first be cold. I need to chill the environment and then climb under heavy, hygge blankets of finest fleece. This makes perfect sense.

In my wild, younger days before the counseling, I kept the house very, very cold. Like 68. Are you horrified? You are thinking, "Well, I guess we know why the other relationship didn't work out." I eventually realized that was prohibitively expensive, not to mention terrible for the environment. It's morally flawed to smugly carry my little reusable bag to Publix and come home to bask in an icy tundra powered by the energy of a private jet. I know this.

Air conditioning just may be the tragic flaw of the comfortable world. We are Macbeth, cold, deranged and unstoppable. A few years back, the federal program Energy Star suggested people keep their homes set to 78 during the day and 82 at night, which sounds like a Turkish bath. This report was promptly ratioed by the internet.

My husband likes to keep the temperature steady at 73, though I think he is being nice to me and would prefer to set it higher. Usually, I can live with 73. The other day, the one we talked about, I could not. I knocked it down to 71 and hissed at him like a bog witch. We went to bed.

The next evening, on our walk, I once again accessed maturity and remembered to follow up. I delivered a speech I'd prepared. Friends, the best way to not turn something into a whole big thing is to start every screed with, "I don't want to turn this into a whole big thing..."

To wit:

"I don't want to turn this into a whole big thing, but I need you to know I am a woman of (redacted age). My estrogen is going crazy, hormones out of control. I burst into random sweats at weird times. I gain and lose 5 pounds in the course of one afternoon. I am a disaster. Sometimes I am just going to have to turn the thermostat down, and that's the way it is. I'll try to remember to turn it back up later."

"OK," he said.

We walked quietly along the neighborhood duck pond. I was warm and red. I am always warm and red.

"I turned it back to 73 before bed," I said.

"I turned it to 72 when I woke up," he said.

"I know."

About the Author

Stephanie Hayes is a columnist with the Tampa Bay Times and syndicated via Creators Syndicate, which supplies content to publications worldwide. As a journalist for 20 years, she has received writing prizes from the National Headliner Awards, Green Eyeshade Awards, the Society for Features Journalism and the Florida Society of News Editors, among others. Her writing has appeared in Chicago Quarterly Review, McSweeney's Internet Tendency and more. She is the author of "Obitchuary," a novel. She lives in Dunedin, Florida with her husband, stepdaughter, enormous cat and tiny dog.

Be Serious: Essays by Stephanie Hayes
is also available as an e-book
for Kindle, Amazon Fire, iPad, Nook and Android
e-readers. Visit creatorspublishing.com to learn
more.

o o o

CREATORS PUBLISHING

We find compelling storytellers and
help them craft their narrative,
distributing their novels and collections
worldwide.

o o o

Made in the USA
Columbia, SC
11 March 2024

32464003R00159